Repairing Your Marriage After His Affair

A Woman's Guide to Hope and Healing

Marcella Bakur Weiner, Ph.D., Ed.D.

Armand DiMele, C.S.W., B.C.D.

THREE RIVERS PRESS • NEW YORK

Published by Three Rivers Press, New York, New York.
Member of the Crown Publishing Group, a division of Random House, Inc.
www.randomhouse.com

THREE RIVERS PRESS and the Tugboat design are registered trademarks of Random House, Inc.

Originally published by Prima Publishing, Roseville, California, in 1998.

Disclaimer: This book conveys the many themes central to repairing a marriage and is based upon our professional experience. The individuals mentioned in its pages, however, are not specific persons but composites, and all names are fictitious.

Printed in the United States of America

Library of Congress Cataloging-in-Publication Data

Weiner, Marcella Bakur.
    Repairing your marriage after his affair : a woman's guide to hope and healing / Marcella Bakur Weiner and Armand DiMele.
        p.   cm.
    Includes index.
        1. Marriage—United States—Psychological aspects. 2. Man–woman relationships—United States. 3. Adultery—United States. 4. Trust—United States. I. DiMele, Armand. II. Title.
    HQ801.D57 1998
306.73'6—dc21   98-28285
                                                                                    CIP

ISBN 0-7615-0963-1

10 9 8

First Edition

To my niece, Judith Paula, whose loving heart helps heal the world.

—Marcella Bakur Weiner

To my sisters, Bel Michelle and Anita Marie, for collaborating in our mutual survival of our own broken family.

—Armand DiMele

Contents

Preface

Our initial idea was to write a book for couples—for the men as well as women. Our research, however, reveals that a man who discovers his wife's affair is likely to have either of two reactions. One is to leave his wife. The wound to a man's ego is often so deep that he does not want to face his real feelings. He would rather cut and run. And he does.

The other reaction is to try to work it out. We have found, in our clinical experience, that the man who stays is usually paired with a woman who acts as the dominant force in the marriage. She is the stronger of the two, the one calling the shots. Therefore, the man who chooses to stay with a woman who has "cheated" on him typically has a history of deferring to her idiosyncrasies.

Women, on the other hand, seem more inclined toward empathy and forgiveness. They're also more willing to look at themselves. Women who are not focused on winning, but rather on creating a lasting love, are able to examine their own feelings of inadequacy. Since women, in general, are far more adept than men at exploring their feelings, they are more often prepared to embark on the difficult task of repairing a marriage. We wanted to write a book that would support the courageous journey of repair and address the inevitable pain that goes with it.

When a man gets caught cheating, his impulse is generally to lie. At first, he denies that it ever happened, no matter how strong the evidence. His next lie comes when the truth can no longer be concealed; he claims it was only the one time, that it never happened before, that he was drunk and lost control of himself. Because the wife wants to believe that what she sees is not really true, he often gets away with elaborate excuses. The third lie is that he'll never do it again. What else can he say? He's desperate to get things back in balance. Even if he dislikes his wife and would love to get a divorce, he wants to leave on his own terms rather than be kicked out of the house. He wants to avoid the humiliation of being forced to leave and the hardship of being taken for every cent he has. Finally, he may lie even to himself. The shame of being caught in a deception may elicit a wish to change, but habits are hard to break.

A woman faced with her husband's affair must take control of her own life by examining her feelings and appraising the situation. She has no reason to believe that her husband, who has broken his vow, will not do it again. Thus the future of the relationship cannot be based on promises, but rather on unearthing the causes of the infidelity. The marriage must be rich and full enough that he will *choose,* not just promise, to be faithful. For him, monogamy will be an act of the heart.

This book is addressed to women, but men can read it, too—especially if they want to begin, with their wives, the difficult journey of repair.

Acknowledgments

We are indebted to Arlene Booth and Andrea Rockower, whose creative thinking contributed to an early structuring of this book. Also to Fran Antigone, C.S.W., for her healing visualizations, and B. J. Sanders for her guided meditation exercise. To Deborah Hillman, Ph.D., whose professional and spiritual presence became an ongoing essence, and to Harry L. Wagner, computer expert and editor; our thanks for their good humor and patience.

We are also grateful to psychotherapist Zoë Kronen, C.S.W., for her unique understanding of the loving mind, and also to psychotherapists Anita Joy Eisenberg, C.S.W., and Dr. William Peter Astwood for their expert opinions, encouragement, and support. A special nod goes to Steve Hein, author, traveler, and teacher, whose insights were essential to our chapters on emotional consciousness.

Jamie Miller, our editor, is applauded for her superb and caring work on behalf of this book. And we thank our agent, James Levine, for his vision, faith, and expertise. We also wish to acknowledge Marcella's husband, Will, for his sensitive feedback on this manuscript.

And finally, our heartfelt thanks to all our clients and students, from whom we continually learn.

Introduction

This book is a survival guide for women who discover that their husbands have had an affair. It adopts the view that, in a marriage, fidelity is a premise as well as a promise. The premise is trust—trust that the partners will not betray each other. The promise is that each partner will forsake all others. When the promise is broken, the very premise of the marriage—the sense of trust—is shaken. Whether this trust can be restored becomes the central question for a woman whose husband is having, or has had, an affair.

In response to her pain, the woman may choose one of several paths: ignore the situation, even the score (by having her own affair), separate, get a divorce, or repair the damage. This book addresses the last choice: healing the marriage bond. Ideas are offered to help women sort out their many and varied feelings so they can gain understanding of what may have led to the affair. Understanding the cause, however, is not enough to effect change. Repair requires that the couple establish, perhaps for the first time, a true commitment to the marriage.

One of the first emotions a woman experiences when she discovers her husband's affair is her intense feeling of isolation. Before discovery of his infidelity, she felt connected to her husband. Now the shock, anger, and pain force her to separate from him. She rapidly goes from a "couple" feeling, to a feeling of being only "one." This sudden sense of aloneness, compounded by feelings of disbelief, anger, and fear, makes her yearn for a source of comfort. Most women find the anguish nearly unbearable, especially in the first few days.

Faced with this kind of pain, women may turn to family or friends for support. Mostly, they seek comfort and a reminder that they're not alone. Unfortunately, when people see someone in pain, most think they must offer solutions. This leads to a flood of opinions and advice that rarely soothes. At this time of crisis, when her primary need is to be heard and understood, a woman will be confused by and perhaps resentful of an overabundance of viewpoints.

Though many books have been written on marriage, few address the issue of the discovered affair. Furthermore, those that deal with the subject tend to view women and men as having homogeneous reactions, according to their gender. Actually, the woman who tends to bury her feelings will respond very differently from the woman who is quick to express her emotions. Understanding the motivations and repair potential for both husbands and wives requires recognizing different personality styles.

In *Repairing Your Marriage After His Affair,* we outline basic personality styles of men and women. Understanding your own and your husband's character structure will help you realize the unattended differences that alienate many couples and often lead to affairs. It will also help you assess the chances of saving your marriage. We believe that certain personality pairings have almost no chance of recovering from the breach of the marriage contract. These are clearly spelled out.

But for situations in which repair is possible, this book addresses the essential considerations with specific steps to take for healing. Further chapters explain how to deal with the children during the critical period, and how to minimize the emotional trauma that frequently gets passed on to them. This book also addresses when, if ever, to tell your children about the affair, and how to avoid using them as pawns after the truth has been revealed.

Repairing Your Marriage After His Affair also addresses essential considerations for reestablishing trust, such as how to go from the "me" status of an alienated couple to the essential "we" of a bonded marriage. It teaches couples to identify and strengthen their "emotional resiliency" and proposes specific guidelines for having discussions that aid in the healing process. Included are exercises for couples that are designed to develop mutual trust so that a true commitment of the heart becomes the renewed marriage vow.

The point to grasp now is that you are not powerless. The affair does mark a definite change in your relationship with your husband, but you and he can still decide whether it destroys or strengthens that relationship. Chapter 1 opens with a sympathetic understanding of the shock you're in now, and provides ways of coping with the upheaval and comprehending what has happened.

1

The Discovery

How did this happen?
How long has it been going on?
Does anybody else know?

Who is she?
What does she have that I don't have?

What's wrong with me?
What should I do?
Who should I tell?
Should I tell the kids?
Should I get a lawyer?
How can I ever forgive him?
How can I ever trust him again?
What if my family finds out?
Is it really true?

Maybe it didn't happen.

*Maybe the person who told me is lying
    to me.*
Maybe they are jealous.
Maybe they want us to break up.

I'll get even with him!
I want him to feel this way.
I won't let him near the kids.
I'll tell his boss.

Who is she?
I'll destroy her!
I'll scandalize him.
I'll report him to the IRS.

I should have known.
How will I ever survive this?
My life is over.
I'd rather be dead.

The pain!

*The excruciating pain of the thought that
    he has been intimate,* naked, *with* her.

*They probably laughed together, went out
    together, sat over dinner—he probably
    bought her things, nice things—perfume*

and expensive jewelry. They kissed! *Long, wet, lingering kisses—I can't stand it!*

Did he lie in bed with her and complain about me?

Did he tell her how much better she was to look at, to make love to?

The secret phone calls from home. I had a strange feeling but he said it was nothing. Why was he whispering using that voice? Sometimes he had this sexy voice on the phone and I knew, but I didn't want to know.

I can't sleep.

I can't watch TV—everything reminds me.

I won't let him near me.

I won't let him touch me.

I feel rage even if he brushes against me.

I hate him.

I hate him!

*I don't want him to leave me . . .
   especially to go with her!*

I won't let him go!

I'm afraid.

I'm afraid.

I'm afraid.

Does he love *her?*
It's one thing if he had sex with her . . .
but does he love *her?*

What if it's more than sex?

I'm sick!

I can't stand it!

Almost nothing is as devastating as discovering that your husband is having an affair. As you work through the emotional trauma of betrayal, many of these thoughts haunt you, playing and replaying in your mind. It takes a long time to recover from the shock, and even after you do, you might continue to lie awake at night, trying to sort it out. After the initial pain subsides, however, you will yearn to reclaim some feeling of stability. In order to do that, you'll need to go beyond the fear, confusion, and anger you feel.

Ultimately, the one question you must answer is should you leave or stay in the marriage? And in order to evaluate that complex question and come to a sound, reasonable decision, *you must have a better understanding of yourself, your husband, and what the affair was about.* Many factors have to be weighed, including the social context, your emotional response, and the psychological underpinnings affecting both partners. We will examine these factors in this and upcoming chapters, helping you to come to terms with the affair and offering ways to repair your marriage and put your emotional life back on solid ground.

First, let's begin with a look at some of the dynamics that underlie a man's drive to have an affair.

The Cheating Heart

Seventy-three percent of men who commit adultery do so after two or more *years* of marriage. Another 23 percent of men who have affairs begin them before their first wedding anniversary. Why does a man choose to have a sexual relationship with a woman other than his wife? To get to the heart of the "cheating heart," let's examine how men are raised.

A crucial aspect of a man's upbringing is the way he relates to his mother and his father. A man begins by being close to his mother but, in order to avoid becoming "sissified," he learns to break away and identify with his father. This paternal imprinting takes him into adulthood. His father learned from his father, who learned from his father, and so on as we go back in time in a manner that Freud called "infinite regress." The male values pervasive in American society include these: "Don't be a sissy. Don't cry. Make it in this world. Achieve and be someone." Along with these values is the push to exhibit sexual prowess. Sexual conquest is considered a sign of manhood. Male children are still encouraged to be independent, strong, aggressive, and free of constraints. Furthermore, men, molded into positions of social power, are seen as superior to women. The man is now caught in the web of seeing even his mother as inferior, despite his early attachment to her. Men have power; women do not.

Power

When having an affair, a man wields power. He can see his lover or not, leave his wife or stay, share his money with either or both, and establish all the rules, such as spending weekends only with his wife. One man explains:

> I love both of them, my wife and my lover. They each give me something. My wife is a fine person, very kind. I wasn't madly in love with her when we got married, but there was something so good about her, I felt she was the right one to marry. It's just that the passion has never been there. I love her character and intelligence, but somehow, there's this emptiness inside me, and my lover fills that space. I try not to talk about my wife to my lover because, truth is, I'm not going to leave her and my kids. And my wife, she's somewhat naive, sweet, so if she knows, she's not letting on. It's much better that way. And frankly, it's made my marriage even better. I appreciate my wife much more.

Some men allow their lovers to glimpse their softer side, even though they hide it from their wives:

It's funny. My lover calls me "Cookie" and "Baby," and I
don't seem to mind. In fact, I really like it; but I used to
hate it when my mother called me sweet little names,
and I never let my wife do it. It's just that somehow,
when my lover calls me all these pet names, I still feel
she sees me as the man. That's important.

In general, men feel that the affair confirms their
masculinity. They enjoy that aspect and often believe
that the relationship has no affect on their marriage. If
anything, they view it as a positive element, strengthening the marriage bond.

Marriage

The woman, whether a full-time homemaker or em-
ployed outside the home, is still most often the supervisor of the household. She chooses the daycare centers
for her children, organizes the routines of the home,
and nurtures family members in sickness and health.
This is still predominantly true, even though many men
are assuming some roles that were previously assumed
by women. Yet with all the changes emerging in our society (including an increase in the number of women
having affairs), men tend to "roam" more than women
do. By the same token, girls in general continue to
choose dolls over more mobile toys, even when offered
a choice. Whether this is due to nature or nurture, or
a combination of the two, is a topic of never-ceasing
debate. Yet both sexes feel strongly that marriage is
a desirable situation. Even a man who wanders may
express his belief in matrimony, as does this one:

I very much believe in monogamy and, yes, I have been married three times. I started young and, hopefully, this third one will be the last. I had extramarital affairs, but only in my two bad marriages. For one reason or another, mostly financial, I couldn't leave them when I should have. One of my affairs occurred when my second wife was having an affair. I can't tolerate that so I filed for divorce immediately.

While marriage imparts a sense of security, for some men, a long-term marriage has a paralyzing effect on sex:

I've been married for 20 years. After a while, the responsibilities of making a living and raising a family started to wear things down. A marriage should be vital and exciting, and sex should be like that, too. But the burdens seem to take over, and sex fizzles out. I've just begun an affair this year, and I'm happy (though guilty) about it. I don't know where it will go. I'm just riding it out.

Sexual Fulfillment

While the affair is often the smokescreen to what men really want, when asked about it, they say that sexual fulfillment is the most important component. They say such things as "It makes me feel alive" and "It's a fantasy come true." For many men who have affairs, sexual needs are not being met in their marriage; the affair is a search for sexual satisfaction.

One man, though glad to be married, speaks of his dissatisfaction in the marriage:

There is much I love about my wife, but there are things in our sex life that I'd like to change. I just don't think it's possible. I've tried to suggest them, and it's useless. For one thing, I'd like her to be more aggressive. Sometimes she just lies there like a dead fish, and I'd like to make sex more exciting. What I'm asking for is not way out of line. But, she doesn't want to change anything, and I finally found a woman who will do all the stuff my wife won't. I'm not bragging about it. I wish it didn't have to be that way. But then again, it makes my own marriage more livable. Now I don't complain.

What about the emotional bond between the man and his lover? Research suggests that the more affairs a man has, the less he concentrates on the emotional ties. In the first affair, he makes a connection; there is an emotional bond. As the affairs continue, however, and as he accumulates more and more extramarital experiences, the emotional ties tend to slacken. The desire to feel loved, needed, and understood decreases as a motivation. The affair becomes, instead, an occasion for fun and play; *the marriage is where the emotional work is done.* Men begin the affair convinced that they are in charge, that the power is in their hands. When men begin to feel attachment during an affair, however, they are out of control and the rules cannot be molded as easily.

Though marriage is a relatively "safe" situation, adultery poses all kinds of risks. And because an affair is secret, it allows and encourages experimentation and fantasy. A lover can play a range of roles, such as mother, father, sibling, boss, or colleague. There is no contract for permanence, and within the boundaries of the affair, sexual fulfillment is possible without revealing personal inadequacies. Without emotional ties, and with the option of assuming a persona of one's choice, the affair—for all its danger—has its own element of safety. Playing with sex, fantasy, and a variety of roles, each partner can be to the other all those things for which marriage has neither time nor place. And, because love does not enter the picture (or does so without wearing out its welcome), the affair, per se, is no competition for the marriage.

The Aging Male

Are older men more or less likely to have an affair? First, let's look at how a man's sexuality changes as he ages. When you let go of old stereotypes, you'll hear quite a bit of good news. For one, an older man takes a little longer to obtain a firm erection upon arousal. The advantage to this is that foreplay can unfold at a slower pace, something women of all ages appreciate. The more mature man also has more control over his ejaculation, so intercourse itself can last longer. And although it takes the older man longer to bring his penis back to an erect state after orgasm, the couple can use the time between erections to explore in other ways. Said a 69-year-old married man when asked what, in the sex act, was most important: "I like to have a chance to experience every possibility, ultimately ending in orgasm."

Only when ill health intrudes upon the older man's sexuality does the sex drive markedly decrease. Impotence is not concomitant with aging. On the other hand, medications such as tranquilizers, high blood-pressure drugs, and antidepressants can cause impotence, as can alcohol, stress, and fatigue. What a man's sexual activity is like in middle age is the most important determinant of how his sex life will be in the later years. A 40-year-old man who engages in sex on a regular basis is likely to have a satisfying sex life in his 60s, 70s, and beyond. So do older men have affairs? Yes, and they are often better lovers than when they were younger. Says a 76-year-old man:

> Unequivocally, older men make better lovers. When I was young, my main interest was only in conquest, and my manner and technique were crude. All I cared about was having an orgasm, turning over, and going to sleep. As I got older, my style and personality mellowed. I got interested in pleasing my partner. All the younger women I had affairs with said that I was the best lover they had had—superior to all the younger men. With my wife, the sex had gone into a routine. She just wanted to get it over with. With my lovers, there was a real sense of adventure. Basically, it's not what people think—older men don't have affairs with younger women just because their breasts stand up. It's a wife's lack of spirit and desire for sex that makes a man, like me, choose to have a lover.

Some older men assume a fatherly role with a younger lover. A 78-year-old man explains:

> My affair makes me feel young again. It's an affirmation of life. If nature intended it not to be so, there would

have been no desire in me. I feel it's something that fulfills me in ways I would not give up for the world. In fact, it makes me a better human being and also a better husband, in ways other than sex. It makes me appreciate my wife for all the things we have in common, such as our intellectual and political outlook, and also our values. With my younger lover I definitely play a father role and give her the love, affection, and support she so desperately needs. She looks upon me as the best friend she ever had. I am.

The good news is that the average life span is increasing. In 1900, average life expectancy was 47; today men can expect to live to age 80, women to age 84. We have added over 30 years to our life span in this century. And—myths to the contrary—older people, both men and woman, are sexually active and sophisticated. They were so before the advent of the "new miracle sex drugs."

Marriage is still "till death do us part," yet death has been arriving later and later. It extends the time that a couple stays married to well beyond what was typical in earlier eras. As the population grows older, the occurrence of life-long marriages becomes increasingly rare, and divorce takes place with unprecedented frequency. The 50- or 60-year marriage, which we wistfully look back on, was never really the norm.

Though a 60-year-old man was once perceived to be nearing the end of his life, he is now merely entering another stage. Eagerly looking ahead, he may choose to reject some earlier attachments. These may include his marriage.

All of this has brought about a major change in attitude. In the aftermath of the sexual revolution of the freewheeling 1960s, there seems to have come about a more lasting revolution of rising expectations. Offered a panorama of options in a society where "more" is equated with "better," some men view multiple sexual partners as an entitlement. Feeling entitled, they steer clear of the guilt associated with "cheating." Instead they see themselves as exercising a "right."

The cheating heart was not born that way. Though the sex drive is innate, it need not be diverted from the marriage. Some men do not cheat and would not consider it. Others do. And different men have affairs for different reasons. Knowing what type of man you married will help you make choices for yourself and your marriage. In the next chapter we'll show you what interferes with a man's ability to create a union of the "me" and "we," the essence of the marriage commitment, as well as examine several "types" of men who are prone to having affairs.

2

Men Who Break the Marriage Bond

An affair creates a profound rift in a marriage. The sense of "coupledom," of being a "we," is no longer a binding force, and the wife most likely feels confused and lost. But the seeds for the husband's affair were not sown overnight. To get to the root of the matter, we must look at each person's sense of themselves as well as their sense of what a couple actually is.

The "Me" and the "We"

For each partner in a marriage, there is both a "me" and a "we," a self and a union of two selves. When two "me's" form a "we" in marriage, the "me's" continue to exist; therefore, finding a balance between "me" and "we" is crucial. Just as the "me"—the self—has needs that must be met, so does the "we"—the bond between two people. To understand what happens in a marriage when the husband has an affair, we must look more closely at this sense of "me" and "we."

A man who has an affair has stepped outside the "we" and acted solely from the vantage point of "me." Yet the ability to live in balance between the "me" and the "we" requires a capacity to keep the separate entities in focus. This capacity stems from our early childhood experience with our parents, and if we're not successful in moving from "me" to "we" at this early stage, our ability to balance between them will remain unformed or damaged.

In our earliest months, we inhabit the "me" as a world unto itself; to an infant, nothing exists apart from "me." The mother (or parenting figure) belongs to this all-encompassing self, and the infant—tied to her every move—absorbs her shifting moods. When mother is sad, baby is sad; when she smiles, the cloud lifts. As an infant you experience mother and "me" as one.

In this merged state of awareness, normal at the start of life, mother does not exist as a real person. Her needs, fears, hopes, and desires have every bearing on you, and you desperately need her in order to survive. But sometime after your first year, assuming that all goes well, this basic sense of oneness starts to change. As you're slowly weaned from an undifferentiated union with your mother, you discover that she is, in fact, a separate person.

At the "we" stage, the world no longer revolves around you; it is populated by others, including mother. You learn that mother has a life of her own, and—

unless something went awry—you don't feel abandoned when she pursues it. But sometimes things do go wrong, and this stage is not completed. When the infant is frustrated too much, for too long, the attachment to a sense of "me" is prolonged. To get what he or she needs, a child will cling desperately to his or her parent. In this primitive state, any moving away, the tiniest sign of independence, is a rupture of life support that brings with it the terror of annihilation.

The child eventually learns he or she can depend on no one apart from the self, and the "me" begins to take over. "We" is but a shadow and a distant possibility. In fact, if out of her own need, your mother prolonged your tie with her, you may not develop a sense of "we" at all. Imbued with a feeling that you are the central person in your world, you look toward others to confirm your self-importance. People are there for your pleasure and you'll "serve" them in return.

If, on the other hand, mother sends you off on your own too soon, you get caught somewhere between the "me" and the "we." Your life is an endless search for something to fill the realm that is not quite "me" and not quite "we." And since most of us, when we're lost at sea, find moorings in the known, the person adrift tends to return to "me." Anything that makes you feel more whole, however fleetingly, is welcome—until the emptiness and yearning reappear.

The man who has a series of affairs while married is one such example. He moves back and forth between couplehood and singlehood. For a while he's comfortable with his lover-of-the-moment, and in fact relishes the situation. But, as the affair progresses, his feeling of disappointment reappears. Now he assumes the cynical attitude of "I've only myself to look to. Better to leave her before she leaves me." And so, the cycle continues as he shifts between "me" and the "we," seeking most of his solace in the fragile "me," which is all he feels he owns.

Our society plays a role, too, in promoting the notion of "me," especially in its advocacy of "rugged individualism." In American society, where "finding yourself" is held to be a primary goal, a man is rewarded for climbing his own mountain. For some men, reaching the heights includes the right to have affairs; the marriage vows are just a required ritual. Though the man may have meant them at the time, his belief that nothing should inhibit self-exploration overrides his marriage contract.

When "me" does not coexist with "we," a person is cut off from others, unable to feel connected to the human circle (for, in truth, we are all connected!). Feeling alienated from humankind leads to isolation and the improbable task of filling all your needs and wants by yourself. Joining your heart with others—in the family, at work, and with friends—is the joy of being human. In marriage, which thrives on interdependence, "we" is vital to survival, and its absence creates a fertile ground for infidelity. If either of the partners feels lonely, a "we" has not been established. If one is desperately searching for the "we" and has not found it in the marital pairing, a common response is to plunge into an affair.

An affair is a sexual relationship outside marriage, whether a one-night stand or a 20-year liaison; and although a troubled marriage may never be shattered by an actual affair, other signs point to a tenuous "we"—flirtations, lingering kisses, excessively passionate hugs—gestures that exceed the bounds of approved socializing. Some men who forsake the "we" can learn to embrace it again; for others, the prospects are less encouraging.

Next we'll look at some traits of men who seem prone to have affairs, focusing on the underlying motives.

Men Who Have Affairs

Is there any way to recognize the type of man who will have an affair after he's married? Experience has shown that men who stray have widely varied characters and no single identifying characteristic. It's not really fruitful, then, to wonder whether you picked the "wrong type," or whether, if you'd chosen differently, the whole affair would not have happened. Still, certain traits shared by all men can indicate an inclination toward extramarital adventures—depending on their intensity in a given individual. We will discuss four common traits and what each can mean for the man in whom they play a dominant role.

Hedonism

Pleasure is among the few things in life that is its own reward. For some men, however, pleasure is not an aspect of life, but a way of being—a way of reaffirming that he is alive. For such a person to deny himself a pleasurable opportunity is to deny the very thing that makes his life worth living. Men like this were often raised in an environment of overstimulation. Their five senses were constantly pressed into action. Men who become hedonistic are tantalized by the smell, touch, taste, sound, and sight of the world around them. They are outer-directed, with little awareness of their depths. Some of this may come from premature sexual experiences, possibly within the home. A mother bathing a young boy and being too attentive to his genitalia is a form of overstimulation. So, too, is watching TV or movies that focus on violence and sex. For the hedonist, raised on this kind of excitement, a lack of stimulation is experienced as a form of death. Hedonistic men are in pursuit of constant stimulation—women, wine, drugs, gambling, even the excitement of a fight—to help them feel fully engaged and alive. Peter was a hedonist, and here is his story:

> I was chasing women pretty much all of my life. Somehow I couldn't settle in with just one woman, feeling that with so many flowers in the garden, how could I pick just one rose? Then I met my future wife at a party given by a friend, and I knew right away that she was the perfect woman. We were married three months later, and for a while, life was a bubble. But then, a year later, the twins were born, and the joy began to end. Suddenly she was busy being a mother. I felt like the gates had been shut around me; a part of me was dying. I buried myself in work. And then I met Ginny.

Ginny was the opposite of my wife, in both body and personality; and because we were working together, I saw her every day. Well, one day it happened. It was wonderful, it was new, and it stayed that way for a while. But now I'm beginning to get that old feeling again—the one that says I have to move on to another woman.

Peter has never found a sense of self apart from his sensuality. He has spent his life frantically going from one pleasure to another. As a child, a sense of unrest pervaded his life, and he was always moving on to a new adventure. Although children are naturally curious, it is a sign of deep disquiet when a child moves quickly from experience to experience, never completing anything. Something new is interesting to such children, but a few minutes or seconds later the excitement has worn off. Toy after toy is discarded in the frantic search for novelty. The child reaches to the world with the question, "What else do you have for me?" Pleasures are accumulated, and the inner world is ignored.

Children who do not have quiet times during which to develop their own inner life may become adult seekers of pleasure like Peter. Their five senses define who they are, and their inner being remains unformed, shaped only by continuous outside stimuli. Yet, depending largely on the outer world to feel alive is a bit like chasing the wind. As T. S. Elliot put it: "Each new beginning is a new kind of failure." The wife of such a man must understand that the "failure" is not hers. It derives mostly from his own hopeless search for a self that's missing.

Compartmentalization

To a certain extent, we all share the habit of separating our lives into discrete areas. We don't behave the same way at the office as we do at home. We know the different roles we have to play during the course of a day, and we automatically adjust. Some men, however, do this to excess. They find it perfectly reasonable to lead separate, parallel lives. If they wind up having an affair, they feel confident that they can manage both relationship "A" and "B." They don't see a conflict between the two. They reason that just because they have "B" doesn't mean they value "A" less. Their hope is that the two, like parallel lines, will never meet.

Carl is a compartmentalizer. He may well have learned this strategy as a child, and now he uses it as his primary method of coping with the world. He grew up in a middle-class family that included his parents and a younger sister. His mother went back to teaching when he and his sister were teenagers. His father was an accountant—a mild, orderly man who was conscientious and exacting in all he did. When asked how things were, Carl's father invariably replied: "All is in order. Everything's under control. No problems." This made for a tepid household in which nothing got out of hand. He, quite literally, "managed" his affairs, and family life was no exception. It was run like an accounting system with separate, carefully monitored accounts for everyone. Carl internalized his father's strategy and became a master at using it. As he tells it:

> I met my wife, Ellen, in college. She was not particularly beautiful or cute, but she was smart, a good stu-

dent. I had already decided to follow in my father's footsteps and become an accountant. Ellen was studying to be a math teacher, and we married. It was a good marriage. I have no big complaints, even now. But after seven years and two kids, I met Rosa, who started off as my client. She was sweet, young, and unmarried, and because she was new to the U.S., she needed my help a lot.

Unlike Ellen, who is very competent, Rosa is like a little girl. She looks up to me and asks me to teach her English, shop with her, help her buy a car. Sex is good; and here, too, I'm kind of teaching her. It's hard to say this, but it's actually been going on for about five years. Rosa and I see each other about two or three times a week—meeting at her house or sometimes at a hotel. Once in a while, if I can, I take her along on a business trip. We have separate rooms, of course. We're very careful.

I guess I'm leading a double life. I certainly don't want to hurt Ellen or my kids. I love them and I'm not going to leave. But still, I can't give up Rosa. I'm not sure what it is, but I believe—really I do—that I have everything under control. Ellen and Rosa are two separate "files" in my life. Rosa accepts the fact that I'm married and not about to get divorced, and Ellen doesn't know about Rosa. At times I feel really guilty, but then I ask myself: "Who am I hurting? If I'm able to handle both, why should I give one up?"

Carl is operating outside the family. Coming from a tepid household, his emotions are kept at bay. Nothing gets out of hand. To expose his emotions would mean a loss of control, and for Carl that signals danger. Not only can he not feel his own emotions intensely, but he cannot intuit another person's either. Thus, he is oblivious to his wife's pain, and his own feelings of guilt and discomfort. To feel them would be to attach himself to another and experience a sense of "we." Carl has no real grasp of what's involved in being a "we." He may not feel a loss, but he has reached a false balance. Men who engage in parallel lives have only a vague sense of guilt because they feel that nothing is really out of line. It comes to them as a bitter surprise when the game is exposed and they learn of the damage it's caused.

Manipulation

Some men try to maneuver in the world by telling people what they want to hear, by making up stories that sound plausible. It gives them a great sense of power to manipulate people, and soon it becomes habitual. They often tell stories even when the truth would do just as well since they get such a rush from persuading others to believe them. Because their fabrications are plausible, they easily win their spouses' confidence. They are often pretty successful, for a while anyway, at taking advantage of that trust.

How does someone learn to be a manipulator? One of the primary ways is through inconsistent parenting. When a child cannot trust that his or her parents will stick to what they say and believe, the world has no solid grounding. As a result, the child feels anxious and depressed, and to cover these painful feelings, fanciful but believable, stories are created. Listeners are disarmed as the "manipulator," with charm and seeming sincerity, shifts from story to story. Manny is a manipulator and this was his experience:

My parents were divorced when I was pretty young. Pop had been a heavy drinker and was okay when he was in a good mood, but I never knew when that would be. When he wasn't, I just stayed away. At the beginning, Mom seemed to take it and she made excuses for him. The things she came up with were different every time. I never really knew what was going on with my parents, but it didn't matter much because they divorced when I was about ten. Pop sort of slipped away, and I rarely saw him. Mom was a part-time actress, and there were always a lot of guys hanging around. When they were there, she'd ask me to go stay with my aunt down the block. She said if I was good, she'd buy me something special. Sometimes she did, but mostly she didn't. Mom said each of her boyfriends was great, and I was hoping she'd take just one of them, but she died before that could happen.

I was in high school when I decided to drop out. I got a job as a salesman, and I really liked it. I lied about my age to get the job, but I looked older, and they never checked. Selling was great, and I was a natural at it; I could just tell when a customer was ready to buy. The boss was pleased, and I finally became a supervisor, telling others how to make a sale. Then Jenny came to work in the store. We dated and then we got married. She couldn't have kids, which was just as well. I started fooling around, seeing customers after work, or getting together with someone I'd met somewhere else.

It wasn't the sex that grabbed me. It was "getting them" that I liked. Women are funny. They all want to hear the same thing. They want you to tell them they're special; that you love them, and you'll leave your wife. It was that part that got me going. The same stories seemed to work every time, with just a little twist here and there. But after a while, Jenny was catching on. I remember one time when she said, "You told me you were at the office working late, but then my friend Lee saw you at a restaurant with another woman."

"You'll laugh at this one," I said, "I was hoping it would be a surprise. She's a travel agent I met over dinner because both of us are so busy. Well, Jen, I guess the cat's out of the bag. I'm planning to take you to Paris for our anniversary, and the travel agent was helping me pick hotels." That was a close one, but I figured if Jen pushed for the Paris deal, I'd manage to get out of it somehow. Like the time Jen found lipstick stains on my shirt. I told her I had been holding one of the women at the office who had just found out that her only child had cancer. She bought that one, but some of my lies are not so easy to swallow.

To Manny, life is nothing more than a magic trick, an illusion. His job is to tell a tale and to make it convincing. Manny has little sense of self and no notion of "we," so a quality of unreality pervades his marriage and his life.

Mid-Life Crisis

Any personality type can go through a mid-life crisis, but some personalities are more prone than others to it. Although the "me" is ageless, seemingly immortal, middle age, between 35 and 60, brings inevitable changes to everyone. For men, the signs—such as graying hair and wrinkles—are not as negative as they are for women. Gray hair makes them "distinguished looking," and wrinkles add "character." Men accept these signs, but there's also an Achilles heel: the issue of male potency. As a man approaches 40, he begins to question whether the measure of his maleness—the ability to attract women—will continue to confirm his manhood. This anxiety can come to any personality type, but some men are more prone to it. The key is how the family handled signs of physical change early in life, including how they responded to illness; when Max reached the stage of life at which he feared growing older, he faced a mid-life crisis. But the roots were planted a long time ago.

Max led a princely existence. He had caring, attentive parents who were on hand for their two daughters and son—particularly their only son. His twin brother had died a few minutes after birth so it was then that Max became the center of attention. Though sturdy, he was considered frail, and his mother feared losing him, too. She doted on him, and any cough or sneeze was seen as a sign of illness. Remedy upon remedy was urged upon Max, and as a good and obedient son, he submitted to his mother's loving ministrations. For him, life was a breeze, and he easily jogged through it all. He was handsome, cheerful, and popular with all who met him.

Apart from minor aches and bruises, and the usual growing pains, Max's early life was easy. A diligent student, he went to the college of his choice and entered the profession he wanted. In his mid-20s, to the delight of both families, he married his childhood sweetheart. They had a good marriage and two daughters, whom Max dearly loved.

Then when Max was 50, with a grandchild on the way, things began to change. He loved his wife, Sally, and their sex life was good, but he'd lost his youthful confidence. His tennis game was still okay, but he wasn't as vigorous as he wanted to be, and he started running out of steam more often. The story of his affair is an oft-told tale:

> I met Laura, who was in her early 30s, just a few years older than my eldest daughter. I felt a magnetic pull toward her but stopped myself time after time, thinking, "I can't do this. I've always been faithful to Sally. And Laura's so young. Where can it possibly lead?" And then one day, it happened. We started an affair. We were cautious and discreet. We didn't pretend it was anything more than an affair. I felt young again, revived, potent. Yet I was still committed in my heart to my wife, Sally. She never found out. At least, if she suspected, she kept it quiet. When I bought a gift for Laura, on a holiday or for her birthday, I bought an even larger, more expensive one for Sally. And I bought Sally surprises even when it wasn't her birthday or a special event. "I like to surprise you," I'd tell her, "You deserve it. For all the years of living with me and giving me such joy." And you know, I really meant it.

Max has a strong sense of self, a well-developed "me," but he is subject to human frailties, as are men whose fears from an earlier period are reawakened, particularly at mid-life. In Max's case, his fears of aging and death are assuaged by having a much younger partner, one with whom he feels he can turn back the clock. Max offers wisdom and experience to Laura in exchange for her exuberance and innocence.

The Type Is Not the Whole Man

Are these male "types" beyond repair? Is there hope for a marriage after an affair? The good news is that yes, there is. Within the personality styles of these men lie strengths as well as weaknesses. How they manifest these strengths after their betrayal is exposed depends a lot on how their wife reacts.

Now she has a decision to make. Does she stay or does she leave? Does she plot revenge or dedicate herself to healing her hurt and their marriage? These are questions you're probably facing. Next we'll look at a few ways in which women typically respond when they hear that the marriage vow has been broken.

3

Male and Female Types: When His Actions Meet Your Reactions

You probably thought that you knew yourself and the person you married—but upon discovering the affair, you're not so sure. Now is the time to step back and take stock, to examine those traits in your husband—and in yourself—that might have helped create this situation. It's also time to consider what it means for your future.

Male Types and the Chances for Healing

"What future?" you may ask. "How can I live with someone who has betrayed me?" Well, you may or may not be able to stay in the marriage, but before you make a decision based on your present hurt and anger, consider all the options. One possibility is stressing the positives of your marriage and de-emphasizing the negatives. Let's look at the male traits discussed in chapter 2 and see how they may affect your choices. Later in this chapter we'll match some female types with the male types and see how specific characteristics interact and what the chances are for repairing the marriage in each case.

A Hedonist's Dilemma

We've seen men like Peter who are hooked on pleasure, on a continuous stream of sensual stimuli, to confirm to themselves that they are indeed alive. To get a man like Peter to be truly committed, you will have to help him shift his point of view. He needs to feel the pleasure and value of commitment to a single loving relationship—his marriage. If your mate is hedonistic, and you've learned that he had an affair, two things work in your favor. First, as much as the hedonist seeks pleasure, he also tends to avoid pain. You and the marriage have meant a great deal to him; now he stands to lose both. He is in an unhappy situation, and he wants either to run away or make it better. If you can show him that your intention is to not only heal the wound, but also improve the relationship, he may see your marriage as a new form of pleasure.

Your second advantage is that men, especially pleasure-seeking men, have a strong inclination toward romance. They seldom manifest this with their wives because there's no mystery, no risk. Romance, especially for the pleasure-seeker, lies in the magic and excitement captured through imagination and fantasy. If you bring that element into your marriage, your chances of keeping your man increase significantly. Positive change occurs when joy and excitement enter. This doesn't only mean such obvious ploys as meeting your husband at the door in sexy lingerie. You might also put more time into activities you both enjoy together, such as browsing through antique stores, making love in the middle of the day, or planning a vacation in a faraway place you have never visited. The goal is to restore a sense of fun, romance, and playfulness.

Checking the Little Boxes— for the Compartmentalizer

If your husband has a tendency to compartmentalize, separating life into little boxes, you are faced with a big challenge. You must help him see that in order for the marriage to survive, there is no room for other relationship "boxes." This may be difficult, as he thinks he can manage separate, parallel lives without causing any damage. Carl, our compartmentalizer, explains:

> My relationship, the one I have with my wife, is primary. The one I had with my mistress, now over, was also important. But that was a different story. It was not the same as with my wife. I did not love her the same way or treat her the same way. I can't explain, but it was different. And it always will be. I can't see them as related in any way.

Carl is attempting to maintain a certain kind of control in his life—to cling fiercely to a private core of self that is not accountable to anyone. And except for certain types of women, as we will see later in this chapter, compartmentalizers like Carl have difficulty forming solid, real relationships—in or out of marriage. Leading a parallel life is the very antithesis of a marriage; it is based on satisfying the "me" rather than the "we."

Fabrications—for the Manipulator

We've seen that a manipulator, like Manny, lives in a world of lies and images. Some men find this way of life exciting, but the downside of manipulation is that these men are eventually found out. Then, like the magician whose trick has been exposed, the manipulator who has been caught in an affair has nowhere to go. His stock-in-trade, his credibility, is shattered.

All "secret" affairs are based on acts of deception, and in order to succeed, deception requires trust. When the trust is gone, however, the trick no longer works. You must help the manipulator learn the difference between reality and fiction, a difficult distinction for one who tends to equate them. His focus is on what *passes* as "real," what will be convincing—not on the truth of a situation. If your husband carried on his affair by manipulating your trust, he has a major repair job ahead of him. Although it's doubtful that you can ever give him that same kind of trust again, the chances of healing the situation are still good. That's because the very faults that brought the trouble on can be turned to good advantage.

On some level, Manny and others like him feel that they are all-powerful. They can do everything, be everything, accomplish everything, and they're willing to put a lot of energy into it. If you can help your husband channel his energy and self-confidence in a positive direction, he can learn to achieve his goals without using deception and lies. Of course, you may feel, understandably, that you're being asked to take on more than your share of the burden to bring about change. If this is so, you might suggest—or insist—that he seek professional help if there is to be any chance of saving the marriage.

It's crucial for him to know that he can no longer manipulate you. He may eventually be quite willing to accept that. Underneath all the lying and subterfuge, he probably wants a partner, and what better partner is there than the one who forgives him for his botched trick? He was terrified of getting caught and having to make a quick escape. Now although he is indeed caught, he's allowed to stay.

In the Middle of the Journey— for the Mid-Life Crisis Man

If, like Max, your husband is in a mid-life crisis, he'll need plenty of empathy from you. He's entered a transient period, perhaps lasting only a year or a matter of months, but it's often a time of intense emotional turmoil. Facing what he experiences as the loss of his potency, the symbol of his manhood, the man undergoing this passage may not act like "himself." For a man like Max, aging is a painful sign of mortality, and his focus is on recapturing a vanishing youth. Yet, it seemed to Max that his wife was constantly cutting him down. He says: "I want to go out with the boys." She says: "Can't you stay home?" He wants to buy a Jaguar; she pushes for a practical car. Her attitude represents death to him, and he's looking for life.

If you, his wife, can shift your response to one that's more exciting and enlivening, then your marriage can be more vital than it's been in years. For example, you can validate what he feels and also express yourself when he says that he wants to go out with the boys. You can say: "I know how much you enjoy that. Have fun. But don't forget that we have to get up early." That will show both your delight in his pleasures and your care for his well-being. To someone like Max, that can make all the difference.

In short, your chances of saving your marriage once an affair has come to light depend on the emotional styles of both you and your husband. Repairing the relationship will take work and commitment and a willingness to change on both parts. Next we'll examine some "types" common among women, and we'll see how they mesh with the various male "types."

Women's Reactions to the Affair

Women respond to their husbands' affairs in various ways. They range from "I'm out of here!" to "It will work out. In fact, my marriage will be stronger than ever." If you can identify your own "betrayal reaction" and connect it to your past relationships, you will be better able to see the whole situation and understand what you can do about it. The following women show the range of reactions that are common.

Betty: Quick to Anger, Quick to Recover

Right now, you're probably angry. It's a normal response, yet not everyone gets angry in the same way. If you're like Betty, for instance, your anger is intense, which makes you feel alive. Yet your moods tend to come and go without warning. Normally, you are *very* upset when you're upset, but it seldom lasts long. In a few hours, or at most a few days, you're in a new frame of mind—unless you've been betrayed.

If you are like Betty, when you find out about the affair, you have a difficult time—perhaps the toughest of the different kinds of female reactions. For a while life seemed a tranquil breeze, but now, feeling fury and rejection, you're a volcano erupting. Your self-esteem is sinking like a rock. You long for the safety of a healed marriage or the denial of running away completely. Repairing the marriage is difficult for you because abandonment terrifies you. Your fear brings up feelings of hopelessness and anger. The good part is that these feelings don't persist; their intensity waxes and wanes.

Even if you experience such reactions when faced with your husband's infidelity, you can heal yourself and the marriage. To do so may require looking at your history to examine the foundation for your rage. Perhaps no one calmed your emotional fires and assured you that the flames would not engulf you when you were a child. Here is how Betty described her experience:

> Mom and I never got along. She was so moody. One minute she loved me and the next I was the "bad seed." My younger sister was the good one. I was angry and scared, but when I cried and clung to her, she pushed me away and said I was staining her dress. I would go to my room and watch TV, sometimes for hours, not really caring whether I lived or died. It was a little better with Dad, but still not great. Basically I felt no one was there for me. I once found a cat and kept it out in the backyard, away from everyone. I fed her what I could—scraps from my dinner plate—but one day, a few weeks later, she died. I cried and cried, all by myself. Friends? No. I don't have many. They seem to come and go in my life.

With the help of a skilled therapist, a woman like Betty can explore the roots of her anger and her underlying depression. Separating her past experiences of the early years from the affair in the present will help her achieve focus and direction for her anger. Once her emotions are not overly contaminated by the past, she will be able to decide whether to stay or leave without basing her decision on the intense emotionality of the moment.

Betty, as we have seen, is highly emotional; her shifts in mood come and go, but when she feels she feels with total passion. Impulsive, she is prone to self-damaging behaviors stemming from feelings of boredom or emptiness. Yet she can be kind, giving, and even overly appreciative of another person who shows caring.

If Betty were married to Peter, the hedonist, they would have a chance of repairing the marriage. If Peter can show her pleasures and demonstrate appreciation for her charms with any consistency, she will be ready to stay and repair the marriage. His sincere attempts to point out to her the beauty of the world will be a fresh light coming through the darkened clouds. It will help her fill the huge void within herself and build "structures" she never acquired in life. But first, he must commit to her and to their marriage.

Max and Betty would also have a chance if she recognizes that his mid-life stressors are transient, and that they, like her moods, will pass and fade. That is, they will dissipate if the marriage has been good enough for all the years they have been together. If he recognizes the link between the affair and his fears of aging, and if he pledges that he will not stray, this union could work. Betty's intensity would be a plus for Max because it is also a sense of life. This could help Max alleviate his underlying fears of aging and death. But as Betty sees every act as either "all bad" or "all good," any minor infraction or hint of an affair surfacing again will throw her into the depths of fury and despair. If Max could promise to keep the marital vows—and if he sticks to his pledge—then the marriage has a good chance of working.

Betty and Manny, the manipulator, would have less of a chance. His ability to lie is not as persuasive as he thinks it is. Betty will see through some of his deception, and her emotionality will flare up. Fire will course through her veins. As much as Manny will try to wiggle out of his lies, she will be in too much pain and turmoil to hear him. And he, rather than promising to maintain the marital vows he pledged, will only try to twist and turn every which way, but to no avail. Betty would not buy into Manny's trap of deception. Unless he chooses to make a dramatic change in his life-style, the chances of saving such a marriage are poor. Intense therapy for Manny and/or marital counseling for the two of them could be one solution. Men of Manny's type, however, seldom choose this route.

Betty and Carl, the compartmentalizer, would have a chance of repairing their relationship, but the odds for success are not great. What can work for them is the balance between their two types. Betty's intensity and Carl's control can meet down the middle, with each learning from the other. Carl, with his inability to become deeply feeling, can act as a calming influence on Betty as she vents her emotions. Nevertheless, while Carl seeks to lead a separate life and does not easily commit to anyone, he must vow to remain faithful to Betty—and do it.

Dorothy: Few Expectations

Dorothy is a woman who feels nurtured by very little. She doesn't expect or demand much from anyone. Minimal affection satisfies her expectations of love; she is not looking for a totally bonded "we." One kind word goes a long way with Dorothy, who is known for her sweetness and charm. Healing the marriage after an affair is relatively easy. Because she has a guileless quality and a sense of innocence, she is well liked by others. Her belief system, when shaken, is resilient. Dorothy does not want to be alone; she depends on her husband, and she will do everything to keep the marriage going.

Paired with Peter, the pleasure-seeker, Dorothy would have a good chance of recovering her marriage because she is, in her own way, also focused on pleasure. Intent on pleasing others, she will stay and "make it all better." To a pleasure-seeker such as Peter, her desire to please can be an attractive prospect. With Manny, the manipulator, Dorothy also stands a good chance. Tending to subordinate herself to others for fear of rejection, she will allow Manny to take the lead in recovering their damaged relationship. Since Dorothy has difficulty initiating projects on her own, she will likely choose to stay in the marriage and accept Manny's constant plotting and plans. His dominance bolsters her lack of self-confidence, which will keep the marriage intact at least until she sees her pattern and decides to change.

Dorothy and Carl, the compartmentalizer, also would do well together after the affair—but there is a cost. What does Dorothy really feel inside? What's buried under her overall pleasantness? For sure, there is innocence lost. When Dorothy or her type get wounded, they die a little inside, as if someone took a piece of their soul away. They don't complain; instead, they walk around with this sadness, this wound. Even if they seem to get over it (and are often successful to an extent), where they were capable of 90 percent joy in their lives before the affair, they are now capable of only

80 percent. For them, the betrayal is not utterly devastating because people like Dorothy tend to give away pieces of themselves all the time. So now they've just lost another chunk. No big deal.

If Dorothy wanted to make some real changes, of a deep nature, she would need to find out why she is so pleasing to everyone and why the fear of rejection makes her settle for less than she could be. She would also want to learn how to bring her full sense of who she is into her relationship. That would mean accepting the idea that not everyone will—or has to—like her. She has to realize that the ability to say "No" or "Maybe" will not destroy her, and that separation, which is the ability to say "No," is a necessary and healthy part of life. Once she does that, she may feel differently about her marriage. Perhaps she could still keep it and make it even better than it was.

What happens if Dorothy is married to Max, who struggles with mid-life crisis? Sometimes people like Max feel such an urgency to divorce that they provoke their wives to implacable anger. The typical scenario runs this way: She finds out he has another relationship. She becomes angry and feels vindictive. He seizes the opportunity, and so does his girlfriend, who says, "Leave her now. Be with me." He uses her anger as the chance to break away, and on his way out he says to his wife, "You're crazy!"

In her wounded state, "nice" Dorothy can become stubborn and desperate; she is not going to let him exit easily. She says it straight out: "Please don't leave me! My life is nothing without you. We've been through so much together! We can heal this, too." Because she does not attack or reject him, she may arouse his compassion for her. It can make him stop long enough to feel his inner integrity and, perhaps, a sense of genuine love. It is hard to leave someone who so desperately wants you to stay. Her anger may allow him to maintain his distance, but if she can get to his heartfelt sense of responsibility, he will soften. Putting anger aside allows the healing process to develop naturally. Dorothy and Max can work through the crisis.

Isn't it "right" to feel angry? After all, you have been betrayed, and isn't anger a natural response? Yes, it is important to express all your feelings, including anger. You can convey your anger, but if it doesn't give way to a more cooperative feeling, then you cannot move on to healing the damage. Even though your anger is understandable, you cannot hold on to it without risking everything. You have to let the anger go because, if you show him only your fury, everything in him fights you back. In this state of mind, he will not cooperate with you. No animal in the world makes friends with another who is snarling. So your exchange of anger feeds, in effect, his desire to get away and gives him additional strength to leave. Now he wants his freedom—especially freedom from your anger. But people like Dorothy easily relinquish their anger, which may result in prolonging the marriage. Still, there may be hidden costs.

Claire: Neatness Counts

Claire is another kind of woman, a perfectionist with a keen sense of order and neatness. She prides herself on keeping everything "just so." With Peter, the pleasure-seeker, her chances of recovering after the affair are good. He is rarely organized, but he has the capacity to help her become less restricted; at the same time, she wants him to be "neater." So the pleasure-seeker brings to the marriage a valuable sense of spontaneity while Claire provides an orderly influence. Together they can work toward a new balance, and Peter might find during the process that the task of repairing the marriage is highly pleasurable. Instead of continuously searching for pleasure, he can cultivate his own sense of order that offers beauty and security, and yet does not imprison him.

With Carl, the compartmentalizer, Claire would also have a good chance, but would face problems. Instead of focusing on relationships, Claire is connected to work and productivity. Carl, too, does not get enmeshed in connections with others. Each goes a separate way, avoiding the other's feelings. Both Carl and Claire prefer logic to feelings.

Once Claire learns about the affair, she would like to dispose of the problem as quickly as she can. Nevertheless, decisions are difficult for her. Fears of making mistakes interfere with a quick, decisive, and resolutely executed plan of action. Also, acknowledging to the world that she made a mistake in marrying Carl would leave her highly vulnerable to social criticism. She would avoid that at any cost. Fear of public humiliation, and her strong need to be in control, will probably keep her from leaving the marriage.

Carl and Claire are likely to get over the affair, but the underlying issues do not get addressed. Claire does not express anger directly; instead, she judges both herself and others with excessive conscientiousness. She will strive not to deal with the hurt itself but rather to make the unexamined relationship more orderly. As Carl, too, puts his emotions on the shelf, chances for the marriage surviving, in its way, are good. Understandably, the relationship would be much improved if both Carl and Claire got in touch with their true feelings.

For Claire and Manny, the manipulator, the situation is tough. Discovery of the affair leaves her without an anchor. Although Manny will try many ploys to win Claire back, she sees through his deception. This violates her highly prized sense of morality. The revealed affair also evokes feelings of self-blame, further weakening her spirit. In addition, his continued attempts to pull the wool over her eyes suggests to her that he feels no real remorse. This further indicates to her that he's likely to do it again. She may choose to stay only because she cannot bear making messy decisions, but the deep hurt will dampen her life. Manny, impervious to this and committed to his manipulations, will try to convince her that, indeed, everything is fine. Yet he is ill-suited for any kind of monogamous relationship unless he truly feels a desire to change.

Max, in his mid-life crisis, is a difficult match for Claire. With her tight sense of organization, she is everything that Max is hiding from because to him order represents old age and death. Claire, whose capacity for pure pleasure is limited, gets much satisfaction out of organizing life. She is also pleased when people respond to her way of doing things. When Max expresses a desire, a feeling which to him is freedom, she can accept it and organize it. Should he say, "I want to fly to this exotic place I just heard of and learn some native dances," she can put her logic and fine intellect to work. She can sit down with him and, taking the lead, plan the trip with him detail by detail. While Claire may reject pleasure for its own worth, once she can work for it and see results, it suits her style. Order and freedom can then be partners, and the marriage can be repaired.

Holly: Passionate and Impulsive

Holly is both passionate and emotional. She acts impulsively and her moods come and go with ease. People enjoy being with Holly because she is so alive. Attractive in appearance, which is important to her, and somewhat seductive, she is quick to react and colorful in her speech. The emotions, not the intellect, appeal to her. Holly and her type are overly trusting, sometimes almost naïve, in their relationships. They often make poor judgments, but they don't let this get them down.

Holly is also one of those people who suffer from nightmares, but when she wakes up from one, she goes right back to sleep. Others with the same problem often can't get back to sleep after a bad dream, but Holly and her type can let things pass because they have a great facility for letting go. In general, this type of personality has a better chance of repairing her marriage after an affair.

How does Holly manage with our four types of men? With Peter, our pleasure-seeker, Holly has a good chance because she responds to fun as much as he does. These two can share all kinds of things. Sex, pleasure, enjoyment, and fun are valued by both Holly and Peter. For instance, they can travel together since both find pleasure in new places and things. To Holly, being and remaining attractive is very important, so they can go to places where she can dress up, be seen, be admired, receive compliments, and meet new people. Being on the go is natural for her style. Because she has energy and sexual appetite to spare, she and Peter have a lot in common. They can join each other and focus on having fun, and that is essential to repairing their marriage.

Holly would have to be more sensitive to how quickly Peter becomes bored. Despite the fact that both enjoy pleasures, for a man like Peter, mystery, the unknown, the untraveled excite him most. Constantly on the lookout for new stimuli, he turns from thing to thing, from person to person. His ability to be faithful to one plan or one wife is limited. Holly would not only have to be willing and able, as she is, to engage with him in fun, but also open to creating novelty in their life. And, with little tolerance for bad feelings, Holly could lose the unhappy memory of the affair in a world of refreshingly new and creative activities.

With Carl, the compartmentalizer, Holly would have a harder job. He says to our Holly, "Well, it only happened once." Nevertheless, she's upset because she's lost center-stage, which is so important to her. Moreover, he doesn't take kindly to playing just one role in his repertoire. It is important for Holly to be the focus of attention. For a time, she dramatizes her situation, feeling like a "victim" in a romance novel; but that is short-lived. Her main task in repairing the marriage, however, is to understand how difficult it is for Carl to relinquish his private way of being and truly share his life with another. In effect, her task is to demand that Carl place all his eggs, all his toys, in one basket. She must emphasize that outside relationships will not be tolerated. And, as she is creative and imaginative, she just may be able to persuade Carl that he can get all he really wants from her alone.

Holly's chances, however, are better with someone like Manny. She and the manipulator seem on a better track since her type of person is easy to manipulate. Manny can intuit her needs and spin appropriate stories. He will compliment her, tell her how special she is, how she is the only woman in the world for him, and so on. He not only reads her deepest wishes and desires, but he feeds them, keeping her from anger and depression. To him, exploitation is an easy game, and he does love to play it. Holly wants to believe him, and as long as she gets consistent approval and praise from him, life is a bubble. This may burst as Holly ages, however, either when her appearance may be less seductively appealing than she would like or when Manny lessens his flattery of her. But, for the time being, the odds are as good with Manny the manipulator as they are with Peter the pleasure-seeker.

For Holly, the odds are also good with Max, the man facing a mid-life crisis. People like Max only turn to other women when life at home has become mundane. For someone like Holly, dealing with this is easy.

She can easily generate the spark that will show him the value of his marriage. This will take some effort on Holly's part because she must keep her focus on the energy of his mid-life crisis. She will have to maneuver his fragile ego. If she is willing to take that step, Holly has the resources to make it work. For example, Holly will tell him how good his tennis game is and how youthful his appearance is. Sex will eventually become very important because the most significant factor for a man having an affair in his later years is how potent he feels with the other woman. But this, too, is easy if Holly and Max focus their attention on rejuvenating their bodies.

Workout clubs are excellent pastimes because Max will feel like he has rejoined his youth. So will Holly. One caveat, however: The changes that Holly encourages Max to make must be done with love and caring. Nagging about anything at this fragile time will make him feel trapped in negativity. So it is important that Holly keep her spirits high. Her vitality infuses Max as well as the relationship. After a short while, when the mid-life crisis passes, Max will look back with gratitude that Holly stayed with him, and his love for her will foster a true "we." For Holly, the odds of repairing the marriage are the highest with a partner like Max.

Susan: Reserved and Distant

Susan is self-contained and indifferent to social relationships. Her range of emotional expression is as narrow as her circle of friends. She thrives on solitude and limits the amount of time she spends with others. In marriage, too, she maintains her separateness. She stays on the outside of relationships; passion and intimacy are not important to her. To others, she seems cool and aloof, and she responds indifferently to either praise or criticism.

It's unlikely that Susan will team up with Peter, the pleasure-seeker, in the first place; but if it did happen—if they did marry and there's the affair to consider—the path could go in either of two directions. In the first, she just might dismiss the whole thing and live "outside" the affair as she does with much of her life. In the second, if her sense of justice and morality are highly offended, she may choose to leave and lead a life alone, which would also go along with her personality. If she were to stay, she would need to help Peter get to his truth, and this might prove hard for both of them. Peter is not likely to share with her, and she might not be involved enough to care. So, in general, the odds are "iffy" at best.

With Carl, the compartmentalizer, Susan has a great shot. She feels hurt, but not that much; and he has his separate lives in neat, little boxes. How does she reestablish trust? No problem. She never needed trust all that much anyway. Susan and her type are usually strong, independent women who need and expect little from their men. She can even make deals with Carl such as: "I don't care what you do, as long as I don't know about it." This arrangement can work for both of them since they have chosen two very defined "me's," and a very amorphous "we."

With Max, who's in mid-life crisis, the odds are also very good. Susan can give him enough "space" to live

out his youthful needs. By Susan showing a relative indifference, Max will not feel that he must leave the
marriage. When he gets over his fear of aging, he'll appreciate that she did not react with threats and ultima-
tums. Remembering that mid-life crisis is a transient
state is important. It can happen anywhere between the
ages of about 35 and 60, but lasts only a short while.
Once it passes, if marriages stay intact, the man returns
to the "we" with a new sense of union.

Susan and Manny can make it in their marriage.
Indifference to his affair is likely because Susan does
not get involved in feelings. Manny's manipulations will
be less offensive to her than to some of the other
women. Susan accepts marriage and all that comes with
it passively, as nothing to get excited about. If she does
get upset, she will throw herself into her work because
she is capable of high occupational achievements. As for
Manny, he will stay in his "me" state; with Susan, the
pressure is not on him to change. It is a marriage of separate lives, but it is nonetheless a marriage.

Nancy: Sensitive and Vulnerable

Nancy is the opposite of Susan. When she is wounded,
it goes to the core. Nancy suffers from a lack of self-
esteem, and is sensitive to the opinions of others. The
slightest rejection can evoke a major reaction. It is hard
for her to see her own beauty, her own value, and her
own goodness. She feels unworthy most of the time. A
woman like Nancy gravitates toward abusive men in
marriage. She doesn't feel she deserves any better.

Sometimes—usually after psychotherapy—she se-
lects a man who sees her inner beauty and, in that kind
of relationship, can recover some of her self-worth.
Love relationships are difficult for her, however, as she
is convinced she isn't worthy of them. If her husband
has an affair, she quickly interprets it as what she deserves. A person like Nancy does not react with the rage
and anger that forces a decision about divorce. She can
see herself living with a man who is having an affair because she constantly undermines her own value.

How would Nancy be with Peter? This is a difficult
situation. Nancy needs time and distance to recover;
Peter lives on immediate gratification. If Peter can
manage to postpone his needs and be there for her, they
can work it out.

And with Carl, the compartmentalizer? Nancy can
make it with Carl. Because the situation is only tempo-
rary, he can handle her distancing; he'll just return to
his little boxes. Carl is used to Nancy's self-degradation.
He may put some effort into reassuring her that it was
not her fault, but he will tire of this and place Nancy's
grief into one of the little boxes he always carries.

With Manny, the manipulator, she can do better
because he will feed her just the way she needs to be
fed. He will cloak her in compliments, raise her self-
esteem, and assure her of her importance; and Nancy is
desperate to believe him. The good part is that it will
help her pass through the storm, and it may create a
soothing environment that nurtures real change.

Nancy is not likely to do well with Max. He sees
her constant negativity as an albatross around his neck.

He feels the need to free himself of anything that weighs him down, and if the impulse is strong enough, he will leave. On the other hand, he may respond to her pain with a true sense of caring, but he also could perceive that very caring as a trap.

Therapy

Evaluating whether your marriage has a chance of recovering from the affair is significant if you are considering marital therapy or couple's counseling. But beyond personality pairing, many factors affect a marriage. For example, people who are strongly religious often find divorce impossible. And other aspects of spirituality may have a great effect. What if you feel your husband is your one and only soul mate? How easy can that be to cast aside, even in light of the affair?

For situations in which the chances of repairing the marriage are decent, marriage or couple's therapy can help a great deal. Keep in mind, however, that Manny will be trying to out-fox the therapist, and Carl will not necessarily connect therapeutic insight to the rest of his life. Peter might enjoy the therapy because he might find it exciting. Max doesn't want to hear about mid-life crisis since he is afraid of shattering the youthful feeling he only recently rediscovered.

Similarly, Betty, Dorothy, Claire, Holly, Nancy, and Susan will feel as comfortable in therapy as they are willing to be introspective. Getting to know yourself on a deeper level, and having a nonjudgmental and empathetic listener trained in helping others, can be a boon to your marriage. You should realize, however, that couple's therapy does not only focus on the sins of the husband. Marital therapy uses the affair as a way of revealing the underpinnings of the relationship, which open up the psyches of both husband and wife. If you do not want to take any responsibility for the fact that your husband had an affair, then marital therapy is probably not a good idea. But therapy is not the only avenue open to you. If you use this painful time as an opportunity to learn about yourself, you will emerge stronger, with wisdom that will surely serve you in the future.

4

Coping with Betrayal

In the last two chapters, we considered some traits of men who have affairs, and we explored how they are likely to interact—once the affair has been discovered—with wives of various emotional "types." Here we want to examine your private reaction when you are faced with the knowledge of what has happened. Now that the affair is out in the open, how it ultimately plays out depends much on you, the aggrieved wife. Although you may not feel like taking the lead when everything seems so overwhelming, your response to the discovery will affect the actions of everyone involved. Leading the way is important, and spending time thinking about yourself before you try to manage the crisis is crucial. If you simply give in to depression and self-pity, or if you follow vindictive instincts, you can mar your chances of healing the marriage, or of starting afresh with yourself.

Meeting the Challenge

An estimated half of the U. S. population is involved in some kind of marital infidelity. Few experiences are more soul-wrenching or character-testing than being betrayed by someone you trusted. Many common deceptions involve issues of money or power, but the betrayal of a marriage touches the core of self. The discovery does not always mean the end of a marriage; the majority of couples survive the affair. In fact, many couples look back on the incident as a needed wake-up call; they found their relationship strengthened as a result. This is not to minimize your present hurt, but rather to put it in perspective.

You can begin your healing process by considering how you have dealt with betrayal in the past. This will help you see yourself more clearly. Three internal factors can impede your recovery after your spouse's affair:

- Self-blame
- The tendency to view the affair as punishment
- Your own past history of betrayal

Self-blame can strip you of all your strength. Not only is it self-defeating, but it makes you lose sight of the bigger picture. Blaming yourself can render you powerless and paralyze your will by making you feel that anything and everything you do is fruitless. You are then left sitting outside yourself, too weak and helpless to do anything to change the situation.

In essence, self-blame is only half right—and the right half of the expression, the blame part—is the mistake. Whether you blame your husband, "the other woman," or yourself, you will not get far in repairing your marriage when your energy focuses on who was wrong. Both blame and self-blame direct your attention toward anger—either at him or at yourself. So what can you do when your mind keeps defaulting to blame? Here is a therapeutic tool you might employ: Consider that blame is only one step before insight, and insight is essential to learning. Holly, who tends to be highly emotional, says it this way:

> When I heard about the affair, I got hysterical. My standard response, right? After I ranted and raved for a while, blaming him, her, and myself for countless hours, I realized that this wasn't getting me anywhere. Then I calmed down a bit and started thinking. I asked myself, "What made him want to be with another woman?" And right away the light bulb went on, and I saw very clearly that it was my screaming and carrying-on that most likely drove him away. He had told me many times that he couldn't take how emotional I get. He complained that I was always operating at a level of 10—nothing below that—whether I was angry, sad, or happy.
>
> He has mentioned more than once how I handled the time he lost his job due to cutbacks in the industry. When he told me about it, instead of paying attention to his pain and fear, I got more worried about myself. I flew off the handle telling him that it was his fault. What he needed was a refuge, a quiet retreat that he could come home to, to lick his wounds. What I gave him was pain-on-pain. This was not the only time my hysterics sent him out to take a walk. He needed a safe place, and it wasn't home. So, in some way, I see how

my overreactions had a large part in his seeking refuge elsewhere.

As soon as I got it, I felt a sinking feeling. I went into a self-blaming depression. Now it was all my fault, but then I realized that this kind of thinking wouldn't get me anywhere either. It was just typical me, swinging from one emotion to the next. But the stakes were too high to allow myself to keep going to the extremes.

Holly was using her feelings of blame and self-blame to see her part in the troubled marriage. Both she and her husband must search beyond the affair for the steps that led to it. Of course, for healing to take place, her husband must also fully accept his responsibility for his actions. Holly's genuine desire to repair her marriage led her past her tendency to go to emotional extremes. Had she not done this, she would have stayed mired in her anger and depression, unable to heal either herself or the marriage. She would also have relieved her husband of the necessity to confront his responsibility for what happened.

Closely allied with blame and self-blame is the equally misguided response of seeing this crisis as punishment for your past misdeeds. Some people, like Dorothy, who are convinced that they deserve no better, see the affair as their lot. Dorothy had originally fallen into the trap of seeing the affair as her punishment, but caught herself in time, as she explains:

At home we were raised very strictly. When we were good, we were rewarded; and when we were bad, we were punished. But even as a kid, I saw it wasn't always fair. My younger sister might say I did something that I hadn't, but I would get a beating nevertheless. If I had denied it, my mother would accuse me of lying and beat me even worse so it wasn't worth the trouble to deny it. I sort of got used to just accepting punishment, and this stayed with me all my life.

So, when I heard of the affair, my first thought was, "This is more of what I deserve"; but I realized that this was the child in me talking. That was my own private wake-up call. I realized this had nothing to do with punishment. It was clear that I had better concentrate on getting my life in order, deciding what to do—whether I should stay or leave and how best to manage the kids, the money, everything. It seemed the only way to go.

It was fortunate for Dorothy that she was able to separate her past from her present. Your past history of betrayals affects the way you experience betrayal now. If you have a lot of repressed feelings based on betrayals in the past, they tend to piggyback on your current reaction. Can you remember a childhood friend who betrayed your trust by gossiping about you? Do you recall swearing a brother or sister to secrecy, only to have them use your secret against you? It gets deeper as you get older. If your parents separate, you might feel betrayed. After all, didn't they promise to always be there for you?

Teachers betray children's confidences by reporting them to parents. Even religious leaders have been known to gossip. As a rule, mothers do not betray you in the same way that lovers, friends, and others do when you are older; yet the death of your mother when you are young can be experienced as the greatest betrayal of your life. If the surviving spouse remarries, the child perceives another betrayal. All of the pain can be mitigated by a loving, caring person who is there for you at the time it takes place—someone who allows you to feel your own reactions without quelling them. Unfortunately, when a child most needs that kind of support, others are involved in denying their own sense of loss. When a child does not feel safe to express hurt, anger, and fear, the pain goes to a corner of the psyche and reappears in later crises.

To free yourself from the baggage of unfelt emotions, you must allow yourself to remember the past and allow the feelings to emerge. They will be painful, but not as painful now as they were then, because you are not as vulnerable as you were as a child. But being able to separate the past pain from the present is vital for dealing with the betrayal.

When you examine your history, pause for a minute or two and try to recall a betrayal associated with each of the following. Remember, you are trying to unblock memories to free yourself from repressed pain. Therefore, allow yourself to spend a little while with each one. Recall a betrayal and allow the feeling to enter. Most people can report at least one betrayal from each of the following categories:

- Mother
- Father
- Sisters or brothers
- Friends
- Teachers in school
- Religious leaders

Dorothy tells it this way:

I was about two when Mom died. She had always been there, and, suddenly, poof, like a cloud of smoke, she was gone. I would look for her, thinking in my two-year-old brain that maybe she was playing hide-'n-seek, as we sometimes did, but she was nowhere. Sometimes my dad or my brother of seven would scoop me up and tell me to stop. No one told me why. When I cried and kept repeating, "Mommy, Mommy, I want my Mommy," they would just quiet me with, "She's not here." They wouldn't tell me why she was gone or when she would be back. Nothing.

When I finally found out that she would never come back, I was devastated. They kept trying to calm me by saying, "Mommy's in heaven, and now we'll have to carry on because it will make her happy." They should have let me cry and face it—I wouldn't be so fearful now.

As we have seen in the preceding chapter, Dorothy does not want to be alone. When someone close to her threatens to leave, it reminds her of her mother's desertion. Thus, no matter what her husband does, Dorothy continues to cling. She simply cannot bear to go through another episode that brings up those painful memories.

Even if you react differently to your husband's affair, it is likely that your past betrayals will come into play. When you recognize this connection, this tie that binds your present to your past, you will gain the freedom to deal with your current situation in a realistic

manner. When you do not make the distinction between past and present pain, they tend to bleed into
one another. Once you have recognized and reconciled
yourself to your past, you are free of its chains and able
to act according to present circumstances.

Anatomy of a Response to Betrayal

Let's examine Nancy's responses when she discovered
her husband's affair. Perhaps you will find them similar
to your own.

> I felt as though I had suddenly been thrown into a bath
> of ice water. Or kicked in the head. My breath was
> knocked out of me. I was in shock. If I had had even a
> dim awareness of what was going on, I kept it buried.
> Now it was real. It was happening. I couldn't believe it.
> But I had to, didn't I?

For many women, including Nancy, the initial response is surprise. This is a natural physical reaction to
a sudden change in one's state, like the startle response
that babies experience when you suddenly toss them a
little too high in the air. Our feelings and emotions help
us survive; they are our body's way of alerting us to the
fact that something is going on that needs attention.
When the wind is knocked out of us, physically or emotionally, we have to get our bearings. We have to move
from asking, "What is happening to me," to making a
judgment about what to do; taking action gets us back
in balance.

The shock of surprise, in particular, tells us that we need more information before we can choose an appropriate course of action. A pleasant surprise, like a birthday party, allows us to recover quite rapidly, "A birthday party just for me? Great!" A painful surprise, as in Nancy's case, will take more time to unravel. In her situation, the thinking goes, "So, now I know the truth. I guess I sensed it but refused to see it. I'm shocked, but I have to do *something*." And she did.

Her story is not unfamiliar, and after the initial shock, she could see that all the evidence had been there for some time. She was a fairly secure, stable person with a firm sense of herself. She had not allowed her suspicions to drive her into fear or panic. She had worried, though, that her husband, Henry, *could* be having an affair, that *maybe* she was gaining too much weight, that *maybe* she was not giving Henry enough attention. Still, she protected herself by denying what she saw, by rationalizing the evidence she faced:

> Maybe I'm just silly in all of this. True, Marge told me he was seen with a much younger woman, but he owns a large business, and it could easily have been a business meeting. That does happen. And, if he seemed to be talking intently to her, maybe they were concluding a deal; there are lots of women in business these days. Maybe she was part of something new and wonderful that was happening to our family. I figured that could be it.

But such denials were soon out of the question. Her husband and another woman were seen at a hotel by caring and reliable friends. They danced and went back to a room. In no way could she stretch that into a business meeting, and Nancy now had to take a long hard look at her marriage, and then act.

If surprise is the first emotion to hit the betrayed partner, it moves quickly to the next phase: disappointment. Suddenly the marriage was not the safe place that Nancy had always thought it was. Though it once provided her with caring, kindness, financial security, and a friend, that trusted friend was no longer there. Nancy was also disappointed in *herself*. What had she done wrong? What did this "other woman" have that she did not? Was she herself not still beautiful? Smart? A good person? A caring wife? "If Henry no longer wants me," she asked herself, "am I worth anything at all?"

Moreover, she had to admit that the whole thing went against everything she believed in. Eighty percent of the American public believe that adultery is wrong; Nancy also held that view. Thus she found Henry's act hard to fathom and had to wonder about her whole value system and its validity. Three disappointments— in her marriage, in Henry, and in herself and her own set of values—threw her way off balance. As these disappointments slowly sank in, they gave way to the next wave of feeling: gray sadness. Nancy was overwhelmed with the realization that something terrible had already happened, and along with whatever else it meant, she knew it had left her with a deep sense of loss.

Loss means having something of value taken away, and the first devastating loss for Nancy was her sense of self-esteem. This cut deeper than her disappointment in herself and the marriage. She experienced the affair as a form of humiliation, an affront to herself. She could not have been the person she thought she was or this would not have happened. Her second loss, of course, was that of her husband, whose affection for another woman had essentially severed his ties with her. Enraged at the thought that she could be so cavalierly cut adrift, Nancy found she could focus her anger and use it to galvanize herself to action. She simply was not about to lose her self-esteem, her moral values, and her marriage that easily. She was not going to let her boat drift aimlessly for long. Her anger gave her the strength to grab for the oars.

Anger can take another direction, too. It can be turned inward, toward the self, which only deepens the sense of helplessness, sadness, and depression. Had Nancy taken this route, it would have sapped her energy to act. But she possessed, even in her turbulent state, a strong, healthy sense of self; and, instead, she opted to turn her anger outward, toward the woman she now regarded as the one who "stole" Henry. Gone were her destructive self-comparisons to the woman, "Is she more beautiful, wiser, sweeter, more generous and caring than I am?" She saw her as an insidious rival, nothing more.

Fury changed her original attitude from "Who is this other person who has *more* than I?" to "How *dare* this other person steal my husband? What kind of woman could she be?" More to the point, she questioned what kind of man would betray her for such a woman? Disgust, that feeling we get when we want to rid ourselves of something not "digestible," washed over

Nancy in waves as she considered this. Finally, she knew that she would have to make a decision either to heal the marriage or to "get rid of it." No one else could make that decision for her.

Dealing with such tangled emotions is no easy task. This is especially true if you have been unable to sort out your feelings. "I don't know. I'm feeling a combination of things—sad, angry, frightened, a mixture." While that may be an apt description, it is difficult to act unless you can develop a clearer focus. For instance, when children feel pain, they cry; it's an involuntary response. By the time we are adults, however, we are aware of our feelings; and, having language, we know how to identify them. We are no longer automatically responding; we have a general understanding of why we feel the way we do.

We often cloud our understanding in adulthood, though, by conjuring up feelings from the past that we associate with our present state. For example, if you experience a feeling of sadness, you may spend too much time mulling over an incident in childhood that made you sad, perhaps a promise that you were to go to the circus that wasn't kept. This is just idle daydreaming, not coping with the reason you are sad now. Thus, at this stage, after having identified your various feelings, it is crucial that you focus on the present.

The situation you are in needs all your faculties and all your best judgment. Stay with your immediate feeling—no matter how painful. Although right now, this may seem unbearable, it will lead you to something new. You may discover some strength or some aspect of yourself that you didn't know you possessed. Come to appreciate the truth in your feelings, and learn to read the message in them.

Determined to face the circumstances of her husband's affair, Nancy did not deny her feelings. She embraced them and allowed them to carry her more deeply into herself. And once she had reached an understanding of her emotional state, she was ready for the next step—to work out a plan of action. Accepting her true feelings had freed Nancy for what was to come.

How Nancy, or any woman in her situation, will now move to heal herself, and possibly her marriage, depends on the kind of person she is and on the type of man she married. In subsequent chapters, we will look at approaches and problems involved in healing after an affair. Having gone through all the steps of drilling down deep into her emotional core, Nancy is now ready for that. First, however, we will address a burning issue that hovers over every affair: the other woman.

5

The Other Woman

Perhaps the "other woman" has become the target for your anger and rage. That is understandable. There is a societal attitude that tends to blame the mistress for the husband's infidelity. Whether your husband succumbed to a seducer is not the issue, however; focusing attention on "the evil siren" is counterproductive right now.

You've discovered that your husband has been intimate with someone else, and you feel an urgency to get details. You have so many questions: "Who is she? How long has it gone on? Where did they meet? How often?" These thoughts turn over and over in your mind and can disrupt everything you do, especially when you are trying to evaluate whether your marriage can be saved. The questions about the other woman will need to be addressed, but this is clearly not the primary issue. What you're really looking for are answers about the nature of *your* relationship with your husband and whether, given the present situation, you can make your marriage work. You need to find common ground between you and him, a foundation on which you can reestablish trust.

The problem is that, if your husband is intent on keeping the marriage, his responses to your questions are shaded by his desire to allay your fears and anger. Whenever you ask for details, he probably asks himself, "What's the best answer I can give so she won't get angry?" He may have no intention of lying to you, and may be totally committed to repairing the marriage, but his desire for calmer waters may lead him to alter the truth.

The bigger questions are: How does he feel about his lover? Will he ever want to see her again? (and if they have been together for a while) How do they separate? Does he simply call and say: "My wife found out. It's over between us. I will not see or speak to you ever again"? Although you may want to view your husband's affair as sexually motivated, most such relationships provide a man with something he felt was not available in the marriage. Perhaps it's a sense of freedom from responsibility or a feeling of youthful vigor. Sex itself is usually only a small part of the attraction. It is not that men who have affairs do not want their marriage, but as they assume more and more responsibility, a part of them, usually a remnant of their adolescence, wants to balance the burden. Often they choose to do this by more rebellious behaviors, such as lying, cheating, secrecy, and seduction. It's less a matter of having sex than of maintaining the thrill of a certain sense of freedom.

By viewing the affair as purely sexual, a woman avoids looking at the part she may have played in encouraging the scenario. For example, a wife who is frustrated with certain habits of her mate may repeatedly criticize him, hoping that constant reminders will get him to change. It doesn't work. Most men are so sensitive to being criticized that they often react by building silent hatred toward the critic. This reaction is probably rooted in their childhood years when they felt berated by their mothers, and the resentment has been carried into adult life.

Men are so averse to criticism that they invented a word, *nagging*, to portray a wife as a witch constantly harping on the husband's deficiencies. Men can be just as critical of their wives, if not more so, but they don't think of it as "nagging." Nagging is something only women do and that men talk about with each other. They share stories about how their wives nag and commiserate with one another in their feelings of resentment. The reason this is important is that once a man perceives his wife as "nagging," he feels justified in hating her.

This hatred leads to what psychologists call "acting out." When people are angry but don't feel safe enough to express the anger directly, they may "act out" the anger by secretly doing things they know would hurt the other person. Having an affair is one form of acting out. When the affair is discovered, the husband is in a double predicament. On the one hand, he may have started it as a way of expressing the anger he felt toward his wife. Now, after the affair is discovered, he is trying to pacify his wife so she will not divorce him. The last thing he wants is to elicit her resentment.

The situation is too explosive, and because his primary goal is to mitigate his wife's anger, he goes along with the idea that his affair was purely sexual. He wasn't able to be honest about his dissatisfactions before, and he certainly will not be willing to bring them up now. So he characterizes his affair as sexual, especially if he sees that this is what his wife prefers to believe. In fact, he will tend to agree with anything his wife says at this time. If she wants to focus on the sexual aspect of the affair, he will go along with it. If she needs to focus on the evil intent of the other woman, he does not challenge her perceptions. Unfortunately, this leads to additional buried resentment, which has a good chance of reappearing later. Keep in mind that his primary goal is to mollify the situation, so when the wife starts talking about the other woman, his tendency is to go along with whatever is most palatable to her.

If, in the privacy of your own mind, you understand your husband's dilemma, you can approach the issue of the other woman in a way that does not lead him to present you with answers that are not true. If you are really willing to explore this issue, you will stand a greater chance of creating a truly trusting and loving relationship. Before going further, we should clarify that infidelity comes in many forms, and each one requires a different healing strategy. A one-time tryst is different from an ongoing affair. Here are common variations, aspects of which may overlap.

Prostitute As Partner

This is, perhaps, the easiest to deal with because there are typically few emotional attachments. A man seeking sexual pleasure with a prostitute is looking for a release from tensions and anxieties without personal involvement. He may also have specific sexual desires that he has kept secret from his wife. The solution is clear—find out what he needs and see whether there is any chance his needs can be fulfilled at home.

Casual Tryst

This refers to a sexual encounter that is usually not repeated. It could happen at a convention, or with someone he meets at a party or bar. Since these encounters involve little or no emotional attachment, it is relatively easy for your husband to keep his commitment to not do this again. It is important, however, to determine whether your husband was drinking when these incidents occurred. If your mate is a heavy drinker, and if his infidelity is tied to his drinking, his promises to you when he is sober will have little meaning when he drinks. The mind influenced by alcohol is very different from the sober mind; they function like different personalities. The person who cheats on his wife while under the influence of drugs or alcohol is not the same as the person who sits in front of you sober, remorseful, and full of promises of fidelity. If your husband drinks to excess, you must deal with the issue of alcoholism head on, remembering always that alcoholism is a problem—but never an excuse for unacceptable behavior.

The Financially Supported Mistress

This is a person with whom your husband has made an arrangement of financial support in exchange for her total availability to him. Severing this relationship is complicated because she is dependent on him for her financial well-being. Many men who stop seeing a mistress offer a lump-sum payment equivalent to about a year of support money. This is something that the wife may object to in principle, but it offers an amicable solution to a complicated relationship.

The Married Woman

If your husband is having an affair with a married woman, there is likely to be an understanding that the affair will automatically end if either mate finds out. A complication arises when the other woman is part of the wife's community. If they are going to cross paths in the neighborhood or at social functions, the wife should strive to maintain a studied coolness, giving only the barest social acknowledgment completely devoid of emotional content; however, in such close circles confrontation is inevitable. This can be part of the healing process, but it should not be the immediate focus; there is plenty of time to work it out later. The pressing need of the moment is to resolve your husband's part in the affair.

The Single Woman

This situation is the most difficult to resolve, especially if the affair has gone on for some time. Once again, although the attraction may seem to center on the sexual aspect, this is rarely the whole story. A woman who discovers that her husband has been having an affair with a single woman gets particularly angry because, in effect, someone has stolen her man. Her rage and anger are frequently directed toward the other woman, and she begins to talk about her in understandably demeaning terms. Your husband is unlikely to contradict you if this happens, because he understands that to oppose you would exacerbate your wrath. Instead he acts as though you are correct in your evaluation of the other woman. Secretly, however, he probably feels otherwise.

How Did He Feel Toward Her?

Most married men who have affairs with unmarried women view themselves as the seducer. Initially their intention was to have a one-time sexual encounter. They are attracted to someone and proceed to do whatever is necessary to get what they want. The man might not even tell her that he is married; and if he does, he may imply that he has a distant relationship with his wife. It is usually after the first sexual exchange that the man decides to build the framework for continuing the affair. He may talk about how unhappy he is in his marriage; but for one reason or another, usually involving children, he says he cannot leave. Throughout the initial stage of the affair, he carefully tailors his responses so his lover will not leave him. He does whatever is necessary to achieve her affection, such as buying gifts, sending flowers, and telephoning as often as he can. He wants to divert her attention from the dead-end nature of the relationship. Rarely does the man consider that she might, on some level, prefer the relationship exactly as it is.

The unmarried woman who has an affair with a married man has her own reasons for making the choice, conscious or unconscious. She may have a history of being with "unavailable" men and may even fear true intimacy. She may also have a need to "win" a man from a mother or sister figure and, on a deeper level, her involvement with him may also reflect her anger at men for being so weak. These are among the possible psychological motives of single women who get involved with married men. They are rarely the "victim" of his seduction. But none of these explanations are important to the man. He has found someone who loves him exactly as he is—she loves him so much that she is willing to make sacrifices just to have him in her life. He tends to think of the other woman as free of all motives but love.

The truth is that a single woman who has an affair with a married man is clearly treading on someone else's sacred ground. No matter how she frames it in her own mind, she is aware that she is doing something wrong. If she decides to believe his reassurances that she is not hurting his marriage, she does that—not because he has really convinced her of it, but because it assuages her guilt. He, on the other hand, is locked into his own perception of her as the innocent.

Of course, *you* are angry with her! She knew what she was doing. No matter how she rationalizes her actions, she was stealing your husband's affections. So your anger toward her is understandable. The problem is that, in your husband's mind, he was the perpetrator, and wants to believe that the other woman was innocent of all questionable intent. As you express your outrage, he may passively seem to agree, but in his mind he believes you are wrong. He will probably hold on to his belief that the other woman's only sin was falling in love with him.

So as you disparage her, he nods in agreement, but inwardly disagrees. This creates a new form of deception at a time when honesty is crucial. Drop the issue of the other woman's intent. Focus on the two of you. Find out what went wrong and what you need to do to heal this relationship.

How Does He End It with Her?

Obviously, he must stop seeing the other woman. However, if the affair has gone on for some time, it is no simple task to end it. Your husband may easily agree to stop all future contact—never speak to her again—but that is probably not going to happen. Entanglements that accumulated over time will have to be worked out, such as what to do with the clothes he left at her place. They may even work in the same office. Keep in mind that if you exact a promise from him that he does not keep, you once again precipitate deception in the marriage.

So if you ask him whether she has contacted him and he thinks you will be angered by the truth, his impulse will be to deny it. There is therefore only one viable solution—you must allow for some contact, but he must not keep it secret. You must also stifle your negative reactions if he tells you that she called. His telling you is an act of integrity, a reflection that he wants everything to be "above board." If you show anger, he will eventually choose not to tell you; furthermore, if you do not control your reaction at those times, you inadvertently direct him to lie.

So how do you reach an agreement about future contact? You need a way of knowing, as you decide whether you want to keep the marriage, that the "other woman" is not an active influence. Having him promise never to speak to her again will not work. The alternative is that he agree to report all contact to you. This is especially important if he and she work at the same place.

When a woman discovers that her husband has betrayed her trust, she needs to find out whether this will become a pattern. Women who realize that their husbands will continue to have affairs generally choose to leave the marriage. Trust is the essence of a good relationship. You must therefore do all you can to be sure the promises that pass between you can realistically be kept. When addressing the issue of contact with the other woman, you and your husband must make your agreements clear. Keep in mind that you may not be alone in considering separation. He may also harbor thoughts of dissolving the marriage. There are no real assurances for the future, especially the long-range future. He may wholeheartedly agree to short-term commitments. Imagine saying something like this:

> I want us to see if we can repair our marriage. I'm not so sure we can. What I need is some assurance that your energy will stay completely focused on us. I would

like you to promise not to initiate any contact with her, other than one letter or phone call to end the relationship. I understand that there may be details to work out and that she may contact you herself. I would like you to promise that if she does, you will tell me about it.

Will He Go Back to Her?

This thought, too, may plague a woman whose husband has had an affair. Many women hold onto their marriages not because they really want their husband, but because they don't want to lose him to the other woman. If you find that you and your husband cannot repair the marriage, he may eventually pursue his extramarital relationship. Statistically, however, women who have affairs with men who are married rarely choose to be with the man once he becomes available. In addition, men who are married find certain women appealing for affairs but do not choose them as long-term partners.

No decisions are easy as you sift through the damage. As we mentioned earlier, however, the ultimate question you must answer for yourself is whether or not to stay in the marriage. We'll discuss this question in detail in the next chapter.

6

To Repair or Not to Repair

Once you have examined your own emotional state and brought yourself to the point of seriously considering the future, you will have *very* mixed feelings about what you should do. You'll certainly find yourself echoing sentiments from Jimmy Durante's famous song, "Did you ever have the feeling that you wanted to go, but still had the feeling that you wanted to stay?"

What are possible motives for wanting to heal or maintain the marriage after the marital vow has been broken? Some stay married to avoid a sense of shame; you don't want to face the community with a failed marriage. You fear being tagged as someone who lost her husband to someone else. What will your relatives, your friends, your parents think? So you lean toward saving the marriage as a way of saving face, but is that a good enough reason? You must ask yourself whether you can reach a *modus vivendi* (practical compromise) with your husband so you will not simply have to swallow your pride in private.

Another incentive may be the belief that your children need both parents, even in a worst-case scenario. Ask yourself this: How would my child feel if his father and I led separate lives in one home? Such arrangements exist, but they too have many drawbacks. Children are sensitive to the lack of closeness between their parents, and they generally don't understand what it means. If, for example, you decide to live together like roommates, with separate bedrooms and no intimacy, that creates a confusing model for your children, who observe other parents talking, touching, kissing. "Why," your child may wonder, "don't my parents like each other?" The resulting fear and confusion carries into adulthood, affecting your child's own intimate relationships.

Then there's the question of loneliness. How do you feel about being alone? Perhaps you think of the singles-bar scene and feel daunted by it, or you dread the thought of sleeping by yourself. You may not want to face our highly couple-oriented society, in which singles are often neglected by married friends. Indeed, being on your own might be such an unfamiliar experience that the prospect is downright frightening.

Perhaps, like many women, you lived with your parents then got married; basically, you never lived alone. Or perhaps you had a brief period on your own after finishing high school or college, but that was a long time ago. The world looks very different to you now. Times have changed, and you're no longer fresh out of school. Nevertheless, many women have divorced, built new lives, and found happiness. An extreme change is always difficult at first, but can also be exciting—a new adventure.

Perhaps the strongest reason you have for wanting to keep your marriage is to maintain a sense of economic security. You've heard (and statistics bear you out) that after a divorce, the man often attains a higher living standard than when he was married, while the opposite is true for his wife. Even for working women who divorce, the situation is difficult. Some must take on the responsibilities of sole breadwinner and parent. Moreover, because alimony and child-support payments are inadequately enforced, it's easy to envision a rough time ahead.

Finally, the most important consideration in the decision to stay or leave will be the nature of your relationship with your husband. Not your relationship now—that's full of hurt, anger, and disappointment—but the kind of relationship you had before this happened. Was it satisfying? Did you love him? If so, do you still love him? When he closes his eyes at night, and you look at him in silence, can you say to yourself, "Yes, I do love him"?

Remember that all other reasons for staying—money, children, avoiding shame before family and friends, and so on—do not transcend your feelings for your husband. They are important to be sure, but they leave love out of the equation. If you still feel that he is the person with whom you want to share your life, your path is clear. Your love will make genuine healing possible, since you now have a powerful motivation to work things out. This is not to say that the process will be

easy, but without a strong motivation, the chances of repairing your marriage are slim. What can you do to
gather your resources and give it your best try?

Some women make the mistake of focusing their
attention on whether he will "cheat" again. They work
to evoke promises and assurances, and they try to find
ways to monitor all their husband's activities. This is
counterproductive. Of course he will reassure you; of
course he will promise; but there are no guarantees.
Just as he has no guarantee that you will not start an affair yourself, you have no way of guaranteeing that he
won't. In fact, he already has shown that he is able to
find a place in his heart and mind where his deception
is acceptable to him. Centering your attention on
whether he will betray your trust again is fruitless at this
time. If you intend to repair the marriage, the focus
must be on making the two of you a "we," perhaps for
the very first time.

You also need a time for grieving. Allow yourself to
feel deeply and to come out of your grief when the time
is right for you. Then, when you're able to breathe
freely again, you can actively move toward love. Each
part of the process has its own timing. This is true of
sex, as well as everything else; you must follow your own
feelings in the matter of sex. Gradually, you will discover when you feel secure enough to hold his hand,
walk with him in the park, and finally begin to trust him
again. The time for each step will come as you rebuild
your lives and get to know each other in a new way.

During this interim period, you may find it hard to
develop trust, especially in regard to your husband's

comings and goings. A man under house arrest wears a collar that keeps him within 50 feet of his house. If he goes beyond that, a beeper goes off and the police come after him. It's understandable that you might be inclined to put your husband on your own form of house arrest, making him more accountable for his time than he was before. If he says, "I'm going bowling Sunday night," you might immediately ask, "And what are you doing afterward?" It's only natural to feel that way, but how does he respond? A man subjected to such scrutiny after an affair is likely to react negatively. He resents the feeling that his "mother" is watching his every move and wondering, "Johnny, what are you doing?" Asking your mate to be accountable for every second of his time is almost sure to prove counterproductive.

How then, do you handle your strong feelings of suspicion? You're either going to trust or not trust him. It's unlikely that fear will prevent your husband from having another affair. It will only make him more cautious and more devious—just what you don't want. The real goal is for him not to have an affair simply because he doesn't feel like having one. To develop this kind of commitment, your husband needs freedom to be who he is. If you treat him like a little boy—restrict him, belittle him, go through his pockets—he will feel controlled by you, and you will lose him. In order to make the marriage work, you have to let go.

"But," you may ask, "how do I do this? How do I let go?" First, let's consider the role of beliefs in shaping behavior—your own behavior and that of others. Rarely do we stop and think about the connection between thought and action; yet the ways we act and the ways we habitually interpret the actions of others are conditioned by our beliefs. For example, if, as a child, you were punished with a physical act such as a slap, it was your parents' way of teaching you to do the right thing. They believed that the shock and the obvious reproof would reverse, or at any rate modify, your behavior. If, on the other hand, your parents were committed to talking it out—giving you a list of reasons why you should not act a certain way—then they relied on appealing to your good sense in order to elicit change. Whatever system was used in the household left a mark on you, and chances are you carried it into adulthood. Woven into your behavior pattern is a set of morals and values that plays a major part in directing your decisions.

Belief systems commonly lead to self-fulfilling prophecies. Often, without being aware of it, we create the very experience that will make a belief come true. Think about it. Imagine you are invited to an evening out with friends, people you have known for a long time. Not really wanting to go, but feeling obliged nonetheless, you accept. While saying "Yes," you are telling yourself, "I'm sure to have a rotten time. No one knows that my marriage is in crisis, and I don't want to expose it. But I'll go anyway, even if I won't enjoy it." So you go and, as expected, have a terrible time. Not anticipating the "good" that might come from the care of friends or the ambiance of the environment, your beliefs about the experience ran their course. Then on the way home, you think, "I knew it. I had an awful time—

just what I expected." What you probably don't see is that you set it up to be negative. Your expectations precluded a positive outcome.

Now suppose that you had thought differently. You could have said to yourself: "I'll go and have a really good time. I can use a little relaxation, a little time with caring people. And whatever I tell them about my situation, I know they will either accept me or, at worst, reveal their own discomfort with my circumstances."

If you believe that your goal for happiness is attainable, you feel hope. If you believe happiness is not possible, you lapse into hopelessness, depression, and despair. You can actually change some of your beliefs and develop a more positive attitude, even in times of crisis, trauma, or stress. Think of something you believe you cannot do now that you've become aware of your husband's affair. For example, you may believe you cannot join friends for an evening out. Notice what pictures, sounds, and feelings come to you as you contemplate this thought. Get into the thought and let it flow freely through you. Stay with it. Don't run from the negativity. Don't make any judgments.

Now think about the belief underlying this thought. Could it be that you believe you don't deserve to have fun at this time? Or do you believe that your friends will see through you and sense that you are "faking it"? Or perhaps you feel that you are imposing on them and that they are only asking you out because they feel sorry for you. The idea is to identify the belief, whatever it might be. Then ask yourself where it came from. Whose voice are you responding to from the past?

Is it your mother's, your father's, that of an aunt or a grandparent? When you have identified the source of the belief, see if you can believe the opposite. For example, if you go out with friends, you will enjoy yourself. Imagine it through pictures, sounds, and feelings. Let go of the negative belief you had and allow the positive to enter.

This exercise may not come easily at first. It means bringing the unconscious to the conscious, bringing to awareness thoughts that were once buried. Then, by deliberately changing the perspective you had in the past, you instill a new way of seeing. In this critical period of your life, when you are deciding what to do, it's important to think carefully through your old beliefs. You and your husband can do this together, or you can do it alone. Whichever approach you take, be sure to pause before you act and review the beliefs that influence the choice you're making. Turn the negatives into positives by changing your point of view. This will enhance your ability to choose, no matter what decisions you make.

Choosing to Enter Therapy

During this period of delicate maneuvering, the question often arises: "Is therapy really necessary for healing to work?" The answer is that therapy may or may not be important, depending on your needs as a couple. Many men who feel pressured by their wives to enter therapy after an affair are dishonest about their extramarital relationship. They feel obliged to say, "I'll never do it again," even though consciously or unconsciously, they do not think they can be monogamous.

A good therapist, trained in marital counseling, will be able to get beyond the man's false promises or self-deceptions to what really bothers him in the marriage. For example, one man said he was cheating on his wife because she would not let him smoke cigars in the house. The cigar was an important symbol of his man-hood, and he gravitated toward a woman who did not mind the smoke, and who even took a puff every time he lit up. The sight of his lover with his cigar between her lips turned him on. Compared to his wife's shout-ing, "Get that disgusting thing out of here," his lover's erotic gesture won him over.

In therapy, the man and his wife found a simple so-lution to the problem. The man got a good air cleaner for their house and built himself a study. He brought his cigar back home. Good therapists do not try to elicit verbal promises of monogamy; they know promises have little meaning unless the underlying conflicts are addressed. Often, a man who has had an affair discovers that he slowly gave up his joy. Perhaps his wife com-plained about his eating habits, and he started sneaking hamburgers after work. Or she told him that the music he loves was giving her a headache. Little by little, he allowed his freedom to be whittled away, and with it his sense of masculinity. Finally, he recaptured all those pieces of himself in the affair. He could smoke without criticism, watch his sports game, listen to the music he loves, read the magazines he most enjoys. He could also have sex, but the thing he wanted most was a place where he could truly be himself. In therapy, he can start to reclaim all the aspects of himself that were lost and, at the same time, develop a loving relationship with his wife.

An affair is often the way a man acts out what is missing in his marriage. Most men are not as willing to express their real feelings as women are. Men tend to take action. One man said he was having an affair because his wife would not have sex with him, or would only rarely. When he pressed her, she told him that she was no longer interested. He accepted that, felt hurt, and went on to an affair. When they both entered therapy, upon the husband's suggestion (which is unusual), the whole scenario unfolded. It was simple. His wife said she could not have sex with him because he came to bed with dirty feet. She also could not tell him. In therapy, the man revealed that he liked to walk barefoot around outside his house before he went to bed. Because he showered every morning, he felt no need to do so again before going to bed. Moreover, he had no clue that his wife objected to this. As they had only bought the house a couple of years ago, this behavior was relatively new. The wife's inability to tell him how she felt was in fact the real issue. When the therapist dealt with that, the marriage was elevated to a new level, and the affair was forsaken.

Couples can try to do this on their own, but it's hard to stay focused and honest. A man may tell his wife that it's not important that he watch the football game, even when that's not how he really feels. Therapy can provide a safe healing space that helps couples stay focused and be honest. When a man resists counseling, his reluctance may be an additional message that something is wrong.

If you do opt for therapy, choose your professional with care. Your marriage has collapsed and you want to know why. You don't just want to patch it together. The affair is a sign that you need extensive—not minor—repair, and professional therapy is one way of getting to the root of the problem. Finally, whether you seek therapy or not, you must both become more aware of yourselves and make conscious choices in your lives.

Not All Marriages Can Be Repaired

Not all marriages can be repaired; sometimes the only solution is to move on. You, the wife, have given it a fair try, but you are left doing all the dancing by yourself. If, for example, your spouse does not want therapy and does not want to hear your complaints, and you have the feeling that for him the marriage is over, you are probably right.

The affair that your husband had, or is having, is a sign that something is wrong, yet the solution may not be saving the marriage. Certain conditions signal that it's time to leave the marriage, and it's in your best interest to stay alert to such warnings. One such condition is cruelty or abuse, whether verbal or physical. Such behavior is not to be tolerated. Sometimes, however, the abuse is insidious, almost unrecognizable. One woman explains:

He was always poking fun at me. Even in company. And when I'd point that out, he'd tell me that he was just joking around, that I had no sense of humor. If I put on a few pounds, he'd call me "Fatso." Then, in front of friends, he'd talk about how very fat women are prizes in some countries, getting a huge dowry because of their weight, but that in the USA he can't get a dime for me. Once, when we were at a friend's house, I ran out of the room. My friend ran after me and told me he was a mean man, and why did I want to go on living with him? I couldn't answer because—honestly—I didn't know why.

Then, sometime later, I found out about the affairs. Not one, not two, but several affairs, all reported by reliable people who had not told me, at first, because they said I had been hurt enough. When I confronted him, he just insulted me, calling me a "fat, stupid bitch." One of my kids was around, and I'd finally had it. I told him I wanted him out of the house or else I was leaving. I wanted a divorce. Enough is enough.

Likewise, a man may make excuses for physical abuse, but it is equally intolerable. He might say that it was necessary to "calm her down," or that she was so out of control he had to slap her, or that he had been drinking and didn't know what he was doing. No matter how the abuse is characterized or explained, it is always unacceptable, except in self-defense. Again, this type of abuse can be presented as "fun."

He decided to try boxing as an exercise, and at first I saw no harm in that. Then he asked me to be his sparring partner. I told him it was not my thing, but he insisted, saying there was no one else around and how could he practice if I refused? So I gave in. We had done different things together—like when we were first married, and he'd put me on the handlebars of his bike and go flying down the street with me. He would pretend to be going into a tree, and it was only after I screamed that he'd swerve the bike in another direction. Of course, one of those times he missed, and I lost a front tooth. It was an accident though, and I got over it.

But the boxing was different. He was nasty with that. He'd really try to hurt. I'd tell him to stop, but he just wouldn't. I'd see this killer look in his eyes, and it freaked me out. So when I heard about the affair, truth is, I was relieved. It gave me a real reason to get out, and I'm glad he's out of my life.

An affair is often a turning point, enabling a woman to say "quits." If your spouse behaves in unacceptable ways with no clear evidence of remorse, in all likelihood the marriage is untenable. At this point, if you have not sought therapy, you may wish to do so. It's certainly worth considering. Working with a therapist can help you understand the reasons you accepted the inappropriate behaviors and strengthen your ability to avoid doing so again.

The next chapter will explore how to deal with the many feelings and emotional upsets that are an inevitable part of the healing process after an affair.

7

Sorting Out Your Feelings

In chapter 3, we spoke of the importance of getting in touch with your feelings. During this interim period, when you are busy trying to work things out with your mate, examining your feelings is crucial. You'll find that, quite often, your emotions either go from bad to worse, or you try to not feel anything at all. Many people become masters at detaching themselves from their feelings. They attempt to get through their unhappiness by "being strong"—denying, repressing, or "stuffing" their emotions. They intellectualize, rationalize, justify, deny, and defend. In this struggle against their emotions, they develop other feelings—feelings that serve to cover up the original ones. If during childhood, for example, you had to face abusive parents, you may have learned to mask the terrible fear by becoming either numb or angry. You may find the same process going on now in your relationship with your husband; you may respond to him by becoming numb or angry. The best way to deal with your feelings, however, is to be aware of and openly acknowledge them. Masking them with false emotions will not do you or your mate any good.

Chapter 7

Developing Awareness

Without being aware of your emotions and what causes them, leading a happy life is impossible. You may be able to lead a productive life, even a successful life (if you define success by your level of status or material worth). But to lead a happy life, you must know what feels good and what does not, as well as what is likely to feel good in the future. To be fully aware of your feelings, you must acknowledge them, accept them, and know what they are; even in times of trauma, you can identify your feelings as they happen. If you don't, you miss the chance to learn from them, to bring them closer to you, and then to let them go. If you ignore your feelings, leaving unhealthy situations is difficult, and you may get stuck in a painful relationship for years.

Some of your feelings may be triggered by what other people do, or by what you think they have done. Consider the following common expressions. Each represents an instance of placing the blame for a feeling on someone else:

"She made me so angry."
"He makes me so jealous."
"He hurt me so much."

You know you are hurt, but you must understand that the feeling of hurt is *yours,* and once you accept what *you* feel, *you* can make a change. Instead of clinging to your jealousy or anger, you can choose to move beyond it and embrace another feeling instead. Remaining in the negative feeling often leads to a defensive response, which is almost always counterproductive. For instance, screaming and yelling at your husband will only provoke him to respond in kind. Anger begets anger or, even worse, anger begets silent resentment.

Is it possible to act otherwise when you feel so strongly? Yes. It is possible for you to listen closely to what the other person is saying, to listen for the real message behind the harshness. Remember that the nasty tone, the insults, the criticism, the contempt all reflect the wounded child within the adult. At this moment, acting over your own internal distress and calling upon your capacity for empathy is important. To be empathic, "to feel with" another person, imagine yourself in the other person's shoes. As an observer, try to get inside your husband's experience and grasp it from his point of view.

Non-Defensive Listening

One way people tend to invalidate each other is by exercising poor listening skills. Listening is the art that keeps couples together, as well as one of the most important elements of business arrangements, friendships, parenting, and marriage. Real listening means hearing not only the words the person is speaking, but also the emotion underlying the words. Real listening is never about refuting facts, proving who's right, or finding faults in logic. Even in the heat of an argument, when your partner is seized by intense emotion, you can listen beyond the anger and hear and respond to the hurt child behind it.

Once an affair is revealed, many couples become absorbed in anger and fixated on the issues at hand. They argue continuously, flinging accusations and blame at each other. They no longer hear what the other has to say nor do they care about the other's pain. They function on a primitive level of attack and counterattack, intending to wound and humiliate each other.

If you recognize yourself and your partner in this description, the only way to repair your marriage is to begin listening to and validating each other. The following exercise was designed to help you learn that skill.

Improving Listening Skills

You and your spouse sit on chairs opposite one another. Bring a list of topics you have both agreed to discuss. The subjects need not be related to you, but choose five or six topics of an interesting and somewhat controversial nature. Some examples are: Abortion, Crime in America, Drug Rehabilitation, Teenage Mothers, and American Policy Overseas. Each of you chooses a topic from the list (you may both choose the same one). The first speaker talks on the chosen subject for about five minutes. No interruptions are allowed. (You may use a timer to keep track of time.) When the speaker is finished, the listener is to do the following:

First report what was said as though you were a reporter for a major newspaper. Report only the facts as you heard them. Then, when you have finished, report what you feel the other person was trying to tell you. What was the real underlying message? Ask for feedback to see how well you reflected him or her. Were you an accurate "mir-ror"? Now reverse roles and do the same thing. Finally, discuss your findings with each other without resentment. Use the exercise as a learning experience, and know that as you keep practicing empathic listening, your skills will im-prove. So will your life.

Cultivating Happiness

We are all aware of our physical needs, our require-ments for survival: food, shelter, water, and so on. But what about our needs for happiness? The list might in-clude the following:

Acceptance	Independence
Accomplishment	Inner peace
Challenge	Knowledge
Competence	Pleasure
Control of our lives	Privacy
Direction	Reassurance
Empowerment	Relaxation
Freedom	Significance
Fulfillment	Usefulness
Growth	Variety

Although our survival needs are few and vary only mini-mally from one human being to another, our happiness needs vary tremendously. They tend to differ less in content than in their relative importance. For example, everyone needs some freedom and some security, but you may need less security and more freedom than another person. Peter, our pleasure-seeker, needs a lot of freedom; Carl, our compartmentalizer, needs a lot of security. Too much "freedom" would make Carl anxious and insecure. By the same token, sensitive and vulnerable Nancy needs a lot of freedom to gain what she wants, to be seen as someone special. Claire finds security in maintaining a more circumscribed world. You and your spouse may have different ideas about your needs and how to fulfill them. You probably never discussed this, except in times of stress when one of you said, "I need this or that from you." To stay in tune with one another, try this exercise.

What Makes You Happy?

You and your partner each take a large sheet of paper, and on the left side of your page, list 20 personal needs for your happiness. Then make two columns to the right of the list and label them "Myself" and "My Partner." Now, using a scale of 1–10, decide what proportion of each need you can fill by yourself, and what proportion will require help from your spouse. For example, you might have the word "fulfillment" on your list, with a 4 under the "Myself" column (the proportion you are able to give to yourself) and a 6 under "My Partner" column (the proportion you need from your spouse).

Finally, discuss each item on both lists with your partner to discover how you can help each other achieve what you both want. Talk about the issues, using specific, concrete examples. Statements like, "I need freedom but can't get enough from you" are not helpful. Instead, a statement such as "In the area of reassurance, I can give myself a 5 but I need the other 5 from you. You could give me this by kissing me and showing me you are happy to be home." Or, "When I am upset and start to yell, I need you to recognize that I am feeling scared. You can do that by not yelling back at me but coming over to me and holding me close. That will ease my pain and make me feel secure."

It is important, in the forgoing exercise, to give the other person direction. Very often, couples get into trouble because one partner is in distress, and the other does not know what to do. Not knowing how to help can cause a person to back away because we tend to avoid uncomfortable feelings. Telling another person what you wish from him or her is most helpful. If the person cares, he or she will listen and take action. If not, the relationship has very likely become unworkable.

We humans are most articulate, using a wide range of words to depict what we want, need, feel, think, sense, and believe. Yet, watch any powerful orator and you will quickly understand that words are not the only way we communicate. Gestures and body movements also carry messages, and you can learn to observe them. For example, if you see two people standing and talking together, notice their body postures. If they are turned toward each other in such a way that they seem to exclude you, you will probably not walk over to join them. But if their stance allows an open space for you to enter, then you will feel comfortable walking over. Our bodies say much, yet we are seldom as aware of our "body language" as we are of our words. To learn how you can express yourself nonverbally, try this with your marital partner.

Expressive Body Language

Sit opposite but close to one another on chairs of equal height. You will be wordlessly conveying a series of emotions: joy, love, sadness, anger, disappointment, ecstasy, fear, and helplessness. To begin the exercise, person "A" extends an arm to the partner, whom we'll call person "B." "B," by using only fingers, climbs along "A's" entire arm and then moves over "A's" face, finally descending once again to the arm. With each of these movements, "A" expresses—without the use of words—the feeling. If you are working with "ecstasy," for example, convey to the other person through your touch how you imagine ecstasy should feel. Do the same for "love," "anger," and the other emotions. Then, "A" and "B" switch roles and do the exercise again.

When you have completed the exercise, talk to each other about what you experienced in taking both roles. Practice empathic listening with each other as you discuss your experience.

The Positive Value of Negative Emotions

All of our so-called negative emotions have some positive value. They can help to guide us toward health and happiness. Indeed, we are all a mixture of feelings, behaviors, and personal tastes. Dorothy, for instance, has a hard time making decisions, but she is most enjoyable to be with; she is generally warm, appealing, and caring.

Susan likes to be alone and can weather rejection. Her love of solitude and study make her a good scientist. In the proper balance, each "negative" can become a positive trait, helping us stay on our own unique path. Don't be angry or ashamed of your feelings, but learn to use them well. They have a lot to teach you about yourself. If we had no fear, no regrets, no guilt, and no sadness, we would hardly be human. Let's look at what we can learn from a few "negative" feelings: fear, guilt, and remorse.

Fear

In the proper amounts, fear protects us from both physical and psychological danger. In excessive amounts, however, it paralyzes us or distorts our perception of reality. It is up to us to capture the positive value in fear without succumbing to its excesses. Your fear is excessive when it prevents you from experiencing the positive feelings in life, such as joy, intimacy, and fulfillment.

Sometimes our fear keeps us from leaving our comfort zones, and we shortchange ourselves and miss opportunities for happiness. Because we fear the unknown and unfamiliar, it is useful to take a close look at our fears and try to identify them. Often, simply identifying them lessens their grip on us. Another thing you might do is look at the belief system underlying a fear you have. For example, a neighbor asks to borrow something from you. You may feel a pang of guilt, but you refuse. Your fear may be: "If I do this once, he's sure to come back again a zillion times. I don't want to be in that position." And so you hold back a kindness, a neighborly gesture of caring, because of an unreal fear.

Obviously, if the neighbor overextends himself, you can handle this by establishing some limits; but holding on to fear, to distortion, prevents you from fully engaging in life.

What are some fears which, under moderation, help us live a better life?

Fear of losing control. Helps us take the steps necessary to regain a sense of control over our lives.

Fear of failure. Helps us accomplish our goals. Helps motivate us to prepare, organize, and persist.

Fear of being alone. Helps us reach compromises with others.

Fear of the unknown. Helps us take reasonable precautions and prevents us from unreasonable risk.

Fear of dependence. Helps us develop our own resources and become self-reliant.

So, what can we do with our so-called negative emotions?

• Accept them
• Listen to them
• Learn from them

Guilt and Remorse

Guilt is often confused with its twin sister: shame. Shame occurs when you feel humiliated by someone, or intrinsically flawed. Guilt is a moral judgment about unacceptable urges; you feel you have violated some internal standard. Guilt is important because it tells you what your ethics and standards are. At the same time, guilt is not an emotion, *per se*. With an emotion comes a bodily sensation, and a "guilty" person may not be in such a physical state. Instead, he or she thinks: "How could I have done that?" Then the person experiences fear of punishment for displaying sexual or aggressive urges, or defends with rationalizations, such as: "What else could I have done?" Guilt gives you the power to do wrong and then to buy off your guilty conscience by saying: "Don't destroy me. Just direct me to some sort of punishment. I'll settle for that."

Just as guilt is often confused with shame, so is it confused with remorse. Remorse is a feeling of having done something that you deeply regret. Now, you may regret that you have lived in your head for too long and not listened to your heart, but that's not remorse. Remorse is what you feel if you lose control and hurt someone. Remorse is one of those built-in mechanisms that keep us from acting on every impulse. Without remorse, or the threat of remorse, we would have very little self-control; we tend to know in advance what behaviors will cause us to feel remorse. Here is an ancient story that illustrates the punishing power of remorse:

> A man had done something that was outlawed in his spiritual community. He went to see his spiritual counselor, anticipating some form of punishment so that he could be cleansed. Instead, the aged sage told him to go home and eat the best meal he could imagine: roast beef, potatoes, salad, wine, and any other favorite foods. Then, when he had completed the meal, he was to go to bed, taking with him the warmest of blankets, the best of pillows, and the most luxurious of sheets.

As he began to eat his superb meal, he thought: "How can I eat all of this delicious food? I am so undeserving of it." But he remembered that he had promised his spiritual mentor not to deny himself these pleasures, and so he finished his meal. He did so by forcing himself to eat and by swallowing every bite as though he were choking on the food. "Rocks would have been easier to digest," he thought to himself. When he went to bed, sinking into its softness, he thought, "I should be sleeping on a bed of nails," and he cried himself to sleep. He felt remorse for what he had done, and no amount of indulgence could spare him the pain of that feeling.

Guilt, on the other hand, exists in the head. Guilt is a thought, not a feeling like remorse is, and although we use guilt to keep ourselves from acting on certain impulses, what we really need are standards, ethics, and a sense of fair play. We need love for our fellow human beings to replace the fear of our guilt. People who become ensnared by guilt believe that if they tell the truth, they will have to live with an enormous sense of shame and remorse. Because they are afraid of expressing their real feelings—anger, fear, and so on—they cover them with a sense of guilt. As a mental construct, guilt is used to mask the underlying feeling, and it's always a signal to look for what lies beneath it.

A man who breaks his marital vows is angry toward his wife and unable to express his anger directly. He thinks that if he expresses his anger, he'll have to walk out. Yet, expressing anger toward someone does not necessarily mean telling the person off and storming out of a room. Voicing anger in a healthy way means telling someone you are angry and staying there until you get your point across—until you've been heard.

Aristotle understood the art of getting angry when he said: "Anyone can become angry. That is easy. But to be angry with the right person, to the right degree, at the right time, for the right purpose, and in the right way, that is not easy."

People who assume too much guilt tend to equate "bad" acts with "bad" people, but the totality of a person is not the same as what the person "does." Behavior is behavior, and is subject to change; a person has qualities of mind and spirit that run much deeper than any single act he or she may commit. A guilt-ridden husband, afraid to leave his wife, often says something like: "I would feel too guilty leaving her" or "I would feel too guilty leaving my children." One of the complexities of guilt is that, behind the mask, there may not only be anger but also caring and attachment. Thus, the "bad" act—leaving—can be seen by the man as a betrayal of love, as well as an expression of anger.

Helping Him Through the Stages of Repair

If your husband knows that he hurt you, and feels remorse for the past, then there is genuine hope for repairing your marriage. It's an opportunity for you, his wife, to step in and be of help. With empathy, you can ask your husband to do five things: examine his standards, apologize, ask for forgiveness, make restitution, and learn from the experience. We will explore each of these stages in turn.

Examining His Standards

Encourage your spouse to ask himself whether the standards he is using to live his life are really his or someone else's standards. Then match your standards with the ones he mentions and see what you both find. If either of you live by an arbitrary standard in which you do not truly believe, then you are using up energy for purposes that aren't really yours. You need to be true to yourself, more consistent with what you believe, more attuned to your own heart.

Apologizing

If your husband feels genuinely sorry for the past, it is appropriate that he apologize. Of the four male types we discussed, Manny the manipulator has the most trouble with this; his apologies are more pragmatic than sincere. An apology, however, must not be just words—the man must believe it, feel it, and act it. This is where you, his wife, can help. By acknowledging the mistakes you feel you have made in the marriage, you can lead him to examine his own more deeply. The following exercise will help you identify and apologize for past mistakes:

Each of you make a list of the things you've done in the past for which you would like to apologize. Write these lists separately and be sure to include both large and small offenses. For example, you might recall the hurt look on

his face the time you mentioned his thinning hair at a din-
ner party. Neither of you ever mentioned it again. Now is
a good time to apologize. The two of you alternate turns,
and as you hear each apology, be sure to accept it; do not
diminish its importance. This sharing will bring you
closer.

Asking for Forgiveness

True healing means forgiving, letting go of the past,
releasing its ability to hurt you. But, you ask, how do I
forgive when I don't feel like forgiving? Any form of
holding on means that you are a slave—to someone or
something. Forgiveness is freedom, a way of repairing
the parts within yourself that were broken, no matter
whose act caused the breakage. Here is what you can
do:

Think of someone for whom you feel an abundance of love.
Bring that person close to you in your mind and heart.
Hold out your hand to them in a sign of welcome. Tell
them that if, at any time, you have unknowingly hurt
them, you ask for their forgiveness. Now, think of some-
one, your spouse, who has hurt you deeply and extend to
him your feelings of warmth and openness. If you have
difficulty doing that, think of cuddling an animal you love,
a child, or someone else who tugs at your heartstrings.
Open the feelings of love within you and return to sensing
the presence of your spouse, and offer him the same com-
passion and warmth.

Now, as you have extended your feelings of compas-
sion toward him, extend them toward yourself, saying:

"May I be free. May my heart be open. May I choose free-
dom over slavery. May I be at peace." If you wish to con-
tinue, open your heart to all the people in your life who,
knowingly or not, have hurt you. Send them your feelings
of love and forgiveness. Feel and stay with the experience
of your loving heart before you return to your routine. Re-
peat this exercise as many times as necessary. It will help
you to be free; bring you to a newer, more heightened
awareness; and enable you to move on with your life in
peace.

What does true forgiveness mean to you, the wife
who has been betrayed? It helps you to eliminate poi-
sons from your system. Researcher Hans Selye has described the toxic effects that negative emotions can
have on the body. Thoughts influence our well-being,
for better or for worse; each thought creates either positive or negative energy. When you're trapped in feelings of resentment, bitterness takes over, and the world
begins to look hostile, uncaring, and indifferent.

You can change this, however, by forgiving with an
open heart. This release of anger and resentment takes
more than mere words; it calls for a shift in perception.
When you do this, you cut the ties that bind you to the
person who has hurt you. Each time you think "He did
this!" or "How could he?" you are strengthening your
attachment to him. Whether you decide to repair or
end your marriage, tying yourself to him in a bond of
hatred is detrimental to your emotional and physical
health. How can you stop yourself from thinking negative thoughts? Try this:

As the thoughts come rushing at you and you feel unable to exercise control, sit down in a chair with arms. Sit up straight, feet together, and close your eyes. Let the thoughts rush at you. Then in a loud voice, full of energy, shout "STOP" and bang your hand hard against the arm of the chair. Feel the energy course through you as you shout. The energy should begin near your groin and travel up through your stomach to your chest, to your neck, and into your mouth. Do this as many times as you need to. It will quell the negativity and cleanse your system so you are ready to forgive and bring more positive energy inside yourself.

Forgiving, welcoming the positive, does not mean that you are a weakling—quite the contrary! It takes strength to forgive and stay with it. As you allow yourself to forgive, you're able to move into a tranquil state. Then you can look at your options logically: counseling, therapy, or seeing an attorney.

Making Restitution

In order to heal, a wound must be carefully tended; a body that's been hurt must have the proper nourishment. Likewise, one requires nurturing to heal from emotional wounds as well. Acknowledging each other's positive attributes is truly soothing at this time. How can each of you, day by day, show appreciation for one another? How can you find something new and remarkable in someone you once took for granted? While you are working the issues through, you must take time every day to honor the other person and show that you truly care. Choose a comfortable place and spend a few minutes of loving time together, away from the noise, away from the children, away from the buzz of life. This will help you restore your spirits and a sense of connection with one another. It's an important part of your healing.

An activity you may both elect for yourselves is to take vows. To do so, each of you make up a set of promises you intend to keep. You, the wife, may wish to include the following:

- I appreciate the chance to rebuild our relationship. I intend to focus on all the good things we have shared together and to forgive you fully, in my heart.
- I will look within myself to see how I can make changes without blaming you. I am taking responsibility for my own choices, my own life. I will try to stay close to you and be sensitive to your needs along with mine.
- If I flounder in my attentiveness to you, I welcome your alerting me to this. I will accept what you say without feeling criticized. It will be an opportunity to learn.

When you have written *your* vows, sign them, then give your spouse a copy and keep another copy for yourself. If, at any time, you reach a dead end, re-read your vows. They will refresh your spirit and move you forward.

The spouse who had the affair might include such vows as the following:

- I am deeply grieved for the pain I have caused you in breaking our marital vows. I accept responsibility for that and welcome your forgiveness. I am grateful.
- I respect my "fire," but when it threatens to burn out of control, I will be aware and lower it to both our advantage. I will move it into an activity of my choice and/or bring the passion only into our marriage.
- I recognize and accept the fact that the affair was my choice, and I will do all I can to be fully conscious of my behavior, for myself and for others.
- I ask you not to blame yourself for my actions; that only increases my guilt. Instead, just stay close to me as a best friend and I will do this with you, so that we can help one another go through the voyage of healing.

Learning from the Experience

It is important to know ourselves, both our strengths and our limitations. We also need to know what we wish to change in our character to better ourselves. Thinking of the character trait or quality you would most like to change, the one that is in most need of improvement is helpful. Then you can enhance your progress by keeping a daily guide. Under the heading of the quality you've chosen, make a note of what you have done each day to bring about positive change. It can be a small step or a large one.

For the husband who has broken his marriage vow, the trait might be trustworthiness or consistency— any word that accurately describes the conflict he's trying to resolve. Each day, in just a phrase or two, he should write what he is doing about it. As his wife, you too can list a quality you wish to improve in yourself. It may be anger, sadness, lack of forgiveness, or whatever else concerns you. Whatever it is, write down the quality and observe your progress each day. Both partners can do this for several months. Then, if it feels comfortable to you, share the results with each other. Otherwise, simply show your partner through your actions. By these careful steps, you can gradually bring about change, but remember to be gentle with yourself.

You may not always move forward, and that's okay. Try to respect your own pace. Each of you, in his or her own way, has had a hard time; you both need empathy, compassion, and forgiveness. Most of all, extend this kindness to yourself. Take the experience, painful as it was, as a message that you needed to learn. Learn from the experience, and the knowledge you gain will serve both of you well.

Can anyone follow these suggestions? Yes. Do they work for everyone? No. For these ideas to work, you must believe in them wholeheartedly. And, as is stated throughout this book, exercises of any kind suit some people better than other people. For Claire, who is neat, orderly, and attentive to detail, true forgiveness is difficult. This is how Claire describes it:

> I think of myself as a good person. I'm told that I am. And when I heard about the affair and he told me he was sorry, I tried to forgive. But I just couldn't. I couldn't let go. I got stuck in the "What if . . ." part. The theme would replay itself ten, twenty, a hundred

times over: What if I trust him again, and he has another affair? What if he was lying to me all along? What if she is really more attractive than I am? What if he decides to leave me when I'm old? What if he's still seeing her and telling her he will leave me? And then, of course, I found myself throwing all of these "What if's" at him. I hated myself for doing that, but somehow I couldn't help it. I knew it would drive him even further away from me and it did. If there was ever any chance of our marriage working, it's lost now.

Claire held on to her questions, but lost her spouse and marriage in the process.

Intimacy in Marriage

We all yearn to be totally accepted just as we are. We seek this form of unconditional love. We long to be loved even when we are angry, sad, jealous, hurt, or depressed. In fact, when we have the most intense negative feelings, it is usually an indication that we are most in need. Women, more than men, generally are able to ask for what they need since being loved is essential. Men, on the other hand, will often sacrifice closeness to retain their sense of independence. Researchers have found that from the age of two, girls sit closer to each other, look into each other's eyes more often and for longer periods of time than boys do. Boys sit at angles and avoid looking into each other's eyes. This does not mean that they, too, don't want closeness, but that closeness is secondary to independence for most males.

Despite such innate differences, bonding or intimacy is necessary to maintain a healthy marriage. But intimacy can become distorted through such means as jealousy, violence, or loveless sex. A man may feel jealous of his wife if she seems to flirt with another man. The feelings this awakens in him are fears of potential loss, and probably a recapitulation of earlier losses. The loss means a drop in self-esteem since he is no longer king in her eyes, and maybe even signals competition, for another man may be more powerful than he. The childhood drama of mother, son, and father resurfaces.

What is his basic feeling buried under this avalanche of emotions? Fear. He is a frightened child who is about to lose whatever he holds most precious. Unable to contain that pain and look it squarely in the eyes, or take action by talking to his wife about his innermost feelings, he chooses to act angry, petulant, sad. He may even take revenge by choosing another woman, a course of action that loosens and even threatens to break the marital bond. Intimacy has lost its hold.

Jealousy may also lead men to violence. Because men are hesitant to examine their feelings and are trained to *do* rather than *feel,* they are likely to resort to violence when pain, hurt, humiliation, or fear overtake them. The courts hear a multitude of pleas from men, sincerely offered, that "I did it out of love for her." Violence, for them, equates intimacy in that if he didn't care, he wouldn't *do* anything about it. He *acted* and therefore he loves. Of course, this too goes back to earlier times when, as a young boy, he saw pain, hurt, and anguish handled by violence in his household.

Women do not always share their feelings either. A woman like Susan, who rejects closeness out of fear, does not share because she is unaware of her true feelings; they're camouflaged after many years of staying underground. Dorothy, on the other hand, may engage in loveless sex out of fear. Her fear that she will lose her relationship may prompt her to resort to loveless sex as a way of retaining some semblance of intimacy. But it is intimacy distorted by fear. Since intimacy is a form of yielding, she cannot be a free giver when fear rules.

What can you do to preserve the special bond of an intimate marriage? It may be difficult, but the payoff is huge: Accept the negativity within yourself by sharing your innermost self, your deepest fears and desires. And, most crucially, do the same for your spouse. Know that when he seems most obnoxious—jealous, furious, withdrawn—he is feeling fear. It is the child having a temper tantrum because no one truly understands him and no one seems to care. Peer beneath his outlandish behaviors and find what lies beneath. Soothe him as you would pick up and hug the hurt child and kiss the wound to "make it better." And, once you do that, he may no longer need his smokescreen and might be able to reveal his true feelings to you. And, of course, you too must learn to expose your true feelings, not only to him, but also to yourself. Intimacy is not only you with another—it is also you with yourself.

Are all people capable of being intimate? Yes. As babies we all have that capacity. In fact, if we do not experience intimacy very early in life, we die or become depressed. Yet, depending on your environment early on, your need for intimacy may be encouraged or thwarted. People like Susan actually learn to run from true closeness. They receive a clear message: "Don't get too close to people. You'll only get hurt if you do." Especially when they come from people we trust, such as parenting figures, these messages have a powerful effect. This is particularly true if no others, such as older siblings or grandparents, are around to counteract the effect.

Yet change remains possible later in life, regardless of early conditioning. One woman who feared intimacy became aware of her dilemma and described her experience:

> I've always been known as a loner. Even as a kid. Don't laugh, but sometimes I'd play in the closet. Just put some toys in there, close the door, and that would be home. I'm not sure why I did that, and I never told anyone. Most of the time my parents didn't notice. At the times they did notice, they either talked me to death or just ignored me. I got long lectures, but it's funny—I don't remember getting hugged or kissed. When I went away to camp at age 12, my counselor came to kiss me good-night. I gave her my cheek but thought she was really weird. When she tried it the next night, I pretended to be asleep. I stayed alone most of my life.
>
> When I married, it was almost like being alone still. He did his thing, and I did mine. I had an important job, and it took up most of my time. We didn't see each other much or make many demands, and that was just fine with me. Then I found out about this affair. Just out of curiosity, I asked him why. I wasn't really angry; I just

wanted some information. I think knowing things is really important. I was thrown by his answer. It was so unexpected. He told me that I was a cold fish, never interested in him, that I was selfish, self-absorbed, and really quite dull. He said that although we'd been married eight years, he hardly knew me; that I never let anyone get really close to me, including him. He said it was like living in a refrigerator, and he was freezing to death, looking for a warm body, heart, and mind to come home to.

As he told me that, I remembered how I pulled away when my counselor tried to kiss me. She must have felt bad, I thought. So did my husband, for all these years. I decided I didn't want to be that way anymore. For the first time in my life, I was able to hear him, and I sobbed and sobbed. Unbelievably, he held me, and I let him. Our marriage is much better and we love each other, but I still have to catch myself when I start to retreat from other people.

How can you learn to overcome the barriers to intimacy? Remember, no one is born not wanting to be close. You learned to fear nearness, but you can start to move past your fear if you follow these tips that Susan used successfully:

Move toward others with warmth. Begin with a genuine smile while you focus on the other person, holding him or her in the center of your eyes. Stay a moment in that interchange and then continue as feels appropriate, with conversation or with saying good-bye.

Accept warmth when others extend it. Thank them with your eyes, your posture, your welcoming smile, and your words of appreciation. People like to give as well as receive. Allow them to give to you.

Send out signals of trust. People will sense your "vibes." If the message is "Stay away!" they will feel it. Accept each person as an individual and allow yourself to trust. Let your experience with a person be your guide.

Show appreciation for others' good intentions. Do not be afraid to compliment people or show signs of pleasure when they reach out to you.

Make new friends. Take some risks. Show interest in others and reach out to them yourself. You will find that the world is not such a frightening place.

Contribute your time, money, and energy to others. Volunteer; do some good deeds. It not only makes our world a better place, but it also increases your self-esteem when you know that you have made a valuable contribution. Furthermore, doing something positive for others encourages them to seek you out. New friendships are often formed this way.

8

Love and Conflict Resolution

Despite the infinite variety of ways we love and show our love, we all hold something in common. Behind the myriad expressions of love lies a longing for completeness. We search for someone with whom to share our lives, hopes, fears, defeats, and triumphs. We look to love as a means of fulfilling a strong need for attachment. In a long-term, committed relationship, we form a bond with another person, yet remain a separate being. The main difference between a bonded relationship and a fragile short-term one has to do with the couple's ability to weather change. Those in long-term relationships have learned to accept the rhythm of life/death/renewal. Many assets change over the course of a long relationship; yet new qualities develop as well. For example, you both may lose your carefree sense of youth but acquire a shared taste for music or travel.

In a healthy, committed relationship, you don't have to have everything your way or keep all aspects the way they used to be. You accept the fact that your partner is a distinct separate individual. He doesn't experience all the same feelings, think all the same thoughts, or enjoy all the same activities you do. His style of loving is also his own. Love is what makes it possible for long-term relationships to develop new dimensions as they mature, to find new sources of being together as earlier ones fade or become less important.

Although it sounds unromantic, marriage is a kind of business partnership. It's a merger of two separate "companies" that think they can be more productive together than alone. Imagine a simple partnership between, for example, two paper boys selling two different papers to the same houses. If they become partners, one person can deliver both papers, doubling the number of houses the two can cover in the same amount of time Clearly, the partnership is a good idea; but, for it to work, the pair must learn about each other's preferences and needs. What if one person likes to wake up late in the morning and the other wakes early but likes to finish early in the day? It's simple. One delivers early; the other delivers late. On that score, everyone is happy.

Other problems may emerge that aren't so easy to resolve. Suppose, for example, that the boys have a flourishing paper route and one needs to make a schedule change. Do they dissolve the relationship? Many love partners bail out at the first sign of trouble, but good business partners don't quit. They understand how valuable the business is to them, and they work on solving problems. In fact, when a company runs into hard times and adjusts to the new challenges, the company is considered to be well managed and is likely to stay successful. Good relationships are like that, and sensing the value of the marriage for each of them, both partners work to keep it going, even through hard times.

How do you assess the value of your marriage after a betrayal? Once the affair has been revealed to you, likely your first instinct is to run—sometimes to hit and run, but to run in any case. The marriage in this new light doesn't look valuable. If you know yourself, however, and you understand your husband's type, you'll have a good sense of whether you can rescue the company from its crisis. So, before you opt to run, think hard about your choices and look for the underlying message. Even your most horrendous difficulties are sent to you for a purpose—to inform, to challenge, and to help you re-define your choices and needs. Betrayal, infidelity, boredom, mid-life crisis, the frenetic search for pleasure—all are signs that something in your marriage needs healing. If you once had a loving relationship, even early in the marriage, you may do well to consider how to repair what has happened.

Love Rekindled

Love has many faces. At one age we may need one kind of love; at another age, love means something else. In a marriage that works, the pattern of change differs for each partner, and both are able to appreciate and applaud the continuous metamorphosis. But sometimes one partner changes and has no one with whom to share the experience. This is what happened to one man:

I feel like I'm 16 again. That's when I first fell in love. I guess I'm a romantic, but it was a glorious feeling. Then slowly, after I got married, it fizzled. I still don't know why. I cared about her and I still do, but the passion—it's just not there. Everything seems to be working on a low flame. I want excitement in my marriage; I hunger for what's out there—not necessarily other women, but new possibilities and adventures. My wife doesn't feel that. She wants a very quiet life, one with a lot of peace. I was left with this flatness inside of me because I had no one who could share my zest for life. Then I found a lover, someone vibrant and strong and ready to climb mountains with me. I fell in love with her passion for life.

The Need to Punish

Women are more accepting of a husband who strays than men are accepting of a wife who has an affair. To many men, a wife's infidelity is an unforgivable act, and they are fiercely punitive about it. Here is one such instance:

My wife had an affair. I could understand if it was a short kind of thing. But it wasn't. It went on for close to a year. I was outraged. I had been duped; made to look like a fool. Some of my friends told me to leave, but I couldn't because of the kids. They're too precious to me. And I couldn't ask "her" to go either—even though that's what I wanted to do. After all, she was their mother. I got even. I have affairs. I don't tell her straight out, but I know she knows. Let her feel the pain. I don't care. She did it to me. Now it's my turn.

Society's Double and Triple Messages

While sexual harassment suits are in the news, so too are glamorized versions of public figures' affairs. We deplore, we condemn, and we are titillated all at once. We scrutinize every little detail, day in and day out, waiting for more and more information. Movies, TV shows, and novels all romanticize love, but the affair gets our devoted attention. Men still consider women "obtainable," the desired "objects" they seek. Beauty, though its image changes from decade to decade, remains the prize, and aging and ordinary looks are devalued. Men and women of all ages accept this and women buy advertised products they believe will heighten their appeal to men. Affairs will continue as sex, beauty, and women's attractiveness to men are treated as commodities divorced from committed love. Yet, despite the barrage of media hype, some men and women don't have affairs. Those who come from families in which a belief system that affairs are wrong is *lived* tend to keep this perspective. They believe that monogamy is the way to go, and if a problem arises in the marriage, it should be worked on. When that is no longer possible, divorce may be the answer, but an extramarital affair is not an acceptable solution.

Marrying Later; Living Longer

As we head into the twenty-first century, people are marrying later and living longer. For some, a last-time fling is the response to fears of aging. Yet the actual affair may more closely resemble a nightmare than the expected fantasy. The disappointment may lead to a reassessment of the marriage. It renews one's appreciation of all that the marriage has to offer and leads to a strengthened commitment. But whatever the cause of the affair, a wife can detect early signs if she uses her five senses.

Picking Up the Cues of an Affair

What specific signs can a woman look for to determine whether her husband's having an affair? Research suggests that men who have had a great deal of premarital sex are more likely to commit adultery than those who have not. The more lovers a man has had before marriage, the greater the possibility that he will continue the pattern after he is married. What can you, the wife, do?

A man's sudden change of behavior is the first clue. You sense that "something is happening"; your intuition knows it. Perhaps he has found someone to whom he is attracted, but an affair has not taken place. Without attacking, you can simply open your heart to him and hear him out. Both men and women can be attracted to someone other than their spouse. It's natural to react to an attractive person. Yet feeling attracted to someone, and acting on it, are two different responses. Encourage your spouse to be open with you and to tell you whether and when he is attracted to another woman. Engage in honest communication.

Discussing with him the temptations at work and elsewhere can create a sense of closeness, which can deflect the need to act on an attraction to another. It also allows you to share a secret. It's something your spouse would ordinarily keep to himself. As Winnie-the-Pooh (created by A. A. Milne) once said, "When . . . you think of things, you sometimes find that a thing which seemed very thingish inside you is quite different when it gets out into the open and has other people looking at it."

Even though affairs are more likely to occur after five years of marriage, the possibility of an affair is there from the beginning. If you are sensitive and attuned to your husband and urge him to share his thoughts and feelings, then you will be able to see the signs and respond with openness and love. You may not be able to prevent the affair from happening, but your loving heart will give you a better chance of preserving your monogamous relationship.

Guidelines for Talking with Your Spouse

What tools and skills do you need in order to rebuild your marriage? No matter what your personal style— whether you are a woman like Nancy, Dorothy, Claire, or one of the others, and whether your man is like Manny, Max, Peter, or another—all couples need some tools to make their relationship better. If you still feel love and want to preserve and enhance your marriage, here are seven guidelines for talking with your mate. Just participating in a discussion is an act of love, and the following points will help you and your spouse get the most out of any serious talk.

1. **Don't be afraid to talk.** Know that the words "I want to talk to you" automatically engender a defensive reaction. This automatic reaction is triggered by thoughts: "What's wrong?" or, more often, "What did I do wrong?" It's a natural response, probably rooted from a time when your parents were about to chastise you. Because you and your husband tend to see each other as hostile now, discussing a problem with an open mind and heart is difficult at this time. So, try to relax and remember that when your spouse *talks* to you, he *cares* about the relationship.

2. **Deal with one issue at a time.** For example, if you share your feelings about the betrayal, or if he tries to explain why he had the affair, don't broaden the topic to include other issues. Stick to the one problem—the affair—until it is resolved.

3. **Don't bring in examples from the past.** When an experience is recorded in memory, it tends to take on certain distortions. A dream recalled in the middle of the day is different from when you remembered it first thing in the morning. Therefore, if you bring up examples from the past, you and your partner may disagree, and you'll only invite a conflict about whose memory is correct. If you're talking about the betrayal, stay with that and leave out other incidents. Your spouse will hear you better if you don't bring in hurts from the past.

4. **Make an agreement with your spouse.** Establish a pact that if either of you begins to feel irritated or overwhelmed, you can request a pause in the conversation, and the request will be respected. This

doesn't have to be done with words; you can use a symbolic gesture. For example, you might each have an empty glass in front of you, and whoever needs a pause simply turns the glass upside down. It takes self-control to overcome the feelings of the moment, but it's beneficial to both of you not to succumb. The message behind the pause is: "I feel overwhelmed at this moment, and I've lost my loving self in this discussion. Let's pause until I can feel, once again, that I care about you and you care about me." This is a very effective tool to use in discussions, but it takes dedication and discipline to stick with the bargain. It is also important that you stay in the room, no matter how heated the discussion. Leaving the room before it's finished can be devastating to your partner, and you may not be able to pick up the pieces later.

5. **Do not mention or imply ending the relationship.** Even if that's something you're considering, now is not the time to say it. When one feels the threat of abandonment, it creates a sense of panic, and that invites manipulation and deceit. Your partner may try to get you to stay no matter what it takes. (Manny, the manipulator, would have a field day here.) So stick with the issue at hand. The only time to mention leaving is when you are ready to leave; never use it as a threat.

6. **When you've covered one issue successfully, take a break.** Hug each other or shake hands or say "Thank you." One of the most frequent mistakes is to settle one issue then jump to another right away. If you're very emotional, like Holly, you may find

taking a break difficult; yet you'll find a brief "recess" rewarding. If you jump from one issue to another, a difficult discussion may seem endless.

7. **Celebrate.** Following a resolution, buy each other gifts, send a note, go out on the town together. This is called positive reinforcement. It encourages your spouse to work with you at solving problems, and it makes the task less daunting for both of you.

These are some of the techniques that can help couples resolve the conflicts and the issues surrounding infidelity. If you are trying to heal a wound in a relationship, it is important to convey: "What we have together is good. I'd like to make it better. Will you help me to make us better?"

Dealing with Anger

In all probability, anger is among the many feelings you are facing. If you are like the extremely intense Betty, or the impulsive Holly, or the highly sensitive Nancy, or like Dorothy, who is devastated when a relationship ends, you are apt to have trouble with anger. You may be a combination of several of these women, or something altogether different, and still you are in pain—and angry.

Anger is a normal response, and men are no different. Peter will respond angrily if he's denied his pleasures, Max will rage if his true age (and his fears of aging) are emphasized, Manny if his manipulations fail, and Carl if all the boxes he guards so carefully are discovered. We all have our Achilles' heels where anger is concerned. A woman who discovers her husband's affair is understandably angry, but her husband feels anger, too. He is angry about whatever led him to feel constricted in the marriage; angry about the shame and humiliation of being discovered. For both of you, the world is confusing and uncertain right now; and your anger may seem like an insurmountable stumbling block.

It is important to remember, however, that anger is not all negative. In fact, it is much needed. Anger functions as a signal to tell us we don't like what's going on. Anger doesn't go away if we ignore it, deny it, or fail to resolve its cause. It goes "underground," from whence it launches sneak attacks on our health and interpersonal relationships. Buried anger can also surface when the next emotional crisis comes along, intensifying its impact on us.

Although anger is provoked and expressed in different ways, depending on culture, age, sex, personality, and relative power in a situation, the emotion of anger is universal. Most often it begins with a loss or the threat of a loss. Some examples of this are:

Loss of self-esteem. We get angry when we think we've failed or "let ourselves down."

Loss of face. Public exposure of failures or inadequacies can be both humiliating and infuriating.

Loss of valued possessions, skills, or abilities. Losing something that you are attached to can cause both hurt and anger.

Loss of a valued role. If you lose a part of your life that is important to your identity, anger is a natural response.

Loss of valued relationships. We often respond with anger when an important relationship ends.

Now, we'll take a look at the various losses and try to understand them better. We'll begin with loss of esteem—the feeling that one is loved by other people, that one is good and has merit in the eyes of others. Our ideal is to be such a person. Feeling that this has been turned upside down—that we are unloved, helpless, bad—leads us to a great loss of self-esteem. This can occur when the "trauma" of an affair acts as an affront to the self. We fragment and "fall apart."

Loss of face is similar to a loss of esteem, but also involves embarrassment or humiliation. We all have a "public" face and a "private" face. After you learn of the affair, you may feel that your "public" face is damaged. You assume that the world will see you differently now. Extremely sensitive women like Nancy, or very intense ones like Betty, are particularly prone to a punctured image.

Loss of self can also occur with the loss of a valued role. Because many people identify with their titles—doctor, nurse, lawyer, and so on—the loss of such a role entails a loss of self. This also happens when the roles of wife and mother undergo change. Even if you are the one who decides to end your marriage, you still experience loss and, as such, are likely to feel pain.

Marriage is probably among your most cherished relationships. You shared a common life, some common ideals, and all that marriage involves—children, income, home, family, and friends. Now you have lost, or feel you are about to lose, this valued relationship. You're angry, and behind this anger or rage are feelings of loss. You may even sense that you have failed. And although the "evidence" may disprove that, you may harbor some concern about how members of your community will view you. If you are like Betty, who fears abandonment because she can't be alone, or like Dorothy, who dreads being rejected, you are bound to have physical reactions such as a pounding heart, dry mouth, dizziness, headaches, stomach pains, and fatigue.

You may also respond to anger psychologically. A typical response is to focus your attention on your status as the victim and your desire for revenge. This interferes with healing.

Gender roles play a part in how we express anger, as do cultural standards. In some cultures, anger is freely expressed and readily accepted; in others, displays of temper are a serious breach of social convention. In American culture, many men express their anger freely; in fact, it is not uncommon for men to act angry when they feel hurt, afraid, or confused. Angry women, on the other hand, have traditionally been considered "unfeminine." As a result, women are more apt to feel hurt than angry, or to turn their anger into self-criticism and depression. Following are some helpful techniques for handling the bitter accusations that you will most likely face at this difficult time in your marriage.

First, try to understand your spouse's anger. By understanding his motivation, you can often understand what really angers him. In other words, look beyond the aggression, and try to get to the root of it all. Use your sensitivity.

Next, stabilize your partner's emotional state. Use a technique called the "feel-felt-found" approach: "I know how you *feel* about . . . ," "I *felt* that way when . . . ," "I *found* that by doing . . . , things worked out."

And, finally, underreact. To soothe the angry person, maintain a low, even tone of voice and passive body language. Rehearse what you want to say. You'll feel more in control of the actual situation when you deal with your angry spouse (or anyone else, for that matter).

All these suggestions assume that you are in a totally rational and calm state of mind. If you are angry or defensive, being logical is often difficult. The clue to dealing with anger, therefore, is to keep an eye on your energy. If you are filled with rage, wait until the energy has subsided before you attempt a resolution.

When that is done and you have overcome your feelings of anger, you can use, to best advantage, the guidelines outlined in this chapter for talking to your spouse. Knowing that you can disagree with one another without automatically triggering a response of anger, you can move together toward your mutual concerns, again embracing the love and caring you shared in your marriage. The next chapter addresses a central issue for you both—the love and concern you feel for your children.

9

How an Affair Affects the Children

When married couples with children who are dealing with an affair seem to agree to disagree about everything, there is still agreement in one area: concern for their children. They wonder whether their turmoil will have long-lasting effects on their children and whether it will damage the children's ability to love and to trust. They also wonder whether their children will be afraid to have children of their own—afraid of the harm they themselves might cause as parents. All these concerns are valid. For that reason, despite the stress and strain of this difficult time, parents need to stop and think before deciding what to tell their children. Specifically, they need to consider how much, and in what manner, to reveal to the children.

How Parents Help Their Children Develop Self-Esteem

All societies need happy and healthy children. Happy children make good citizens because, later in life, they tend to refrain from antisocial behavior. Basically, happy and healthy children grow up to be adults who generally don't:

Abuse	Explode	Obsess
Attack	Exploit	Overindulge
Blame	Extort	Pressure
Cheat	Force	Pretend
Coerce	Hoard	Rape
Defend	Judge	Repress
Demand	Kill	Steal
Deny	Lie	Victimize
Destroy	Manipulate	Worry

To achieve a feeling of health and well-being, children must develop self-esteem—a sense of their own worth. Our feelings about ourselves, which determine our confidence, our motivation, and our general outlook on life, begin to take shape in the first few years after birth. In fact, our self-concept begins to take form in the first few months of life, when we respond to the world like emotional sponges. Fresh from the womb, we soon feel either wanted or unwanted, loved or unloved, safe or unsafe, cared for or not cared for. Gradually these experiences build a foundation for our self-image, and we see ourselves as good or bad, adequate or inadequate, competent or incompetent, and so on. We learn to sense whether we are liked, respected, trusted.

All these feelings are rooted in the family environment. Later, however, as we venture into the world, our feelings are influenced by the school and social milieu of which we become a part. Our emotional resiliency—our capacity to recover from emotional hurts—is also shaped during our early years. If Dorothy, for example, had more emotional resiliency, she would not be totally devastated by a betrayal. Though wounded, she would be able to return to the security of her self-esteem, to the knowledge that she is a good and worthy person. If our primary needs are adequately met in early childhood, our self-esteem is likely to be high. These needs include the desire to be loved, valued, wanted, respected, and trusted. If these primary needs are not met, self-esteem suffers. Parents, often unknowingly, damage their children by:

- Indirect expressions of emotion (such as silence)
- Disapproving facial expressions
- Angry outbursts ("Do that now, or else!")
- Blaming ("You're always doing the wrong thing.")
- Instilling fear ("Do that again, and I'll send you to live with your Aunt Mary.")
- Creating a sense of hopelessness ("I give up on you.")
- Voicing disappointment ("Why can't you be like Freddy?")
- Conveying a mood of unhappiness ("What a miserable life!")

- Other damaging behaviors such as denial and/or covering up of problems, verbal and physical abuse, violence, and neglect.

Parents, unaware of the strong impact their behavior has on their child, tend to invalidate what he or she is feeling. This can happen even more when a parent is in a state of stress, as results when a spouse's affair is revealed. A child may say, "I feel so bad that Daddy may be leaving us," and her mother thinks, "It's only a child's reaction. She'll soon get over it." Although it's true that the parent is involved in her own deep emotional pain, invalidating her child's equally painful experiences can cause damage. When you invalidate someone, you imply not only that you reject his or her feelings, but also that you consider those feelings abnormal or unimportant. For example, the child might say, "I wish Daddy could always live with us," and the mother might respond, "How could you feel that way?" When our feelings are repudiated in this way, we feel attacked at the deepest level; it's a form of mental and spiritual abuse.

Regardless of whether another person likes or understands your feelings, they are real to you. Those who try to tell you not to feel what you feel are as unrealistic as they are controlling. Often, when a sensitive person is enraged, it is because he or she feels invalidated. Of the various women described earlier, it is Betty, with her passionate and intense emotional range, who most probably felt invalidated early on. Now, a mere hint of criticism, or a suggestion that she act differently, is met with an angry attack.

Children learn by example, of course, but they also intuit things. If their parents are afraid or depressed, children will sense it. Emotions are contagious; so you can grasp the profound effect that parental distress has on children. When we are aware of this effect, and of its impact later in life, we will appreciate the importance of being sensitive to our children's emotional needs. Without neglecting ourselves, we can show our children that we care for them by recognizing their feelings and taking them into account as much as possible. Parents who have a good sense of self-esteem and who have learned to be emotionally resilient demonstrate the following positive attitudes and behaviors toward their children:

Acceptance	Emotional responsibility	Hugging
Affection	Empathy	Joy
Approval	Encouragement	Optimism
Cheerfulness	Enthusiasm	Touching
Confidence	Gratitude	Warmth

You may not be as strong in some as in other of these areas on a given day, but it's important to cultivate them all.

Dealing with Children During a Marital Crisis

Making blanket statements about what to tell children concerning parents' marital difficulties is unrealistic. Children of different ages need different things. Even children of the same age are not necessarily at the same stage of emotional development. Children of any age, however, will sense the disturbance that follows the discovery of an affair, and that awareness must be addressed. Here are some ground rules that parents facing this situation have found helpful:

Rule #1: Never Use Your Children As a Weapon

The very young child, from day one, is sensitive to what goes on in the household. He or she responds to your every mood, and, because the child is an emotional sponge, absorbs everything, creating a lasting effect.

A wife who threatens her husband who has had an affair with "I'll make sure this child knows what kind of a man you are!" is using the child as a weapon. It splits the loyalties of the child, who needs attachment to both parents. Although the child does not understand the situation intellectually, the feeling penetrates distinctly. If Daddy is habitually criticized by Mommy, the child will cringe and move away the moment Daddy tries to offer his affection.

If parents opt to stay in the marriage solely for the sake of the child, they aren't doing him or her a service. The child feels the burden of responsibility for a relationship that, perhaps, should not be. On the other hand, if the wife tells the husband to leave "because the kids would want it that way," she is using the children as a shield to hide her true feelings. Children who are manipulated this way grow up feeling like pawns in a game that is not of their choosing.

Parents sometimes wait until a child is older, perhaps somewhere in the teens, to reveal the "secrets" about Dad's affair. Consciously or not, these people are pleading with the child to side with them, not merely as a matter of moral judgment but also as an act of solidarity. For a young adolescent, who is already struggling with questions of identity and loyalty, this can pose a most traumatic conflict. Children are part of the family; yet an aggrieved wife can feel so upset that she becomes oblivious to the reactions of her child. This is true especially when children are very young and parents think, "What can they know at this age?" But knowing and feeling are an integral part of children's experience, and their behavior will alert you to what is going on in their lives, even as you feel the pain in yours. It may not be easy, but paying close attention to your children's responses and remaining aware of how they are feeling is essential.

Rule #2: A Child Should Always Feel Loved, Not Abandoned

Although it's natural for you to feel abandoned in the aftermath of an affair, it's important that children feel loved and protected throughout the crisis. No matter what the circumstances, they depend on your unconditional love, which is based on who they are—your children. By loving them consistently, you will help them weather the storm and grow up feeling confident in their own ability to love.

Rule #3: Your Children Don't Have to Know Everything

Living in a society where everyone is encouraged to "let it all hang out" and where the media push people to reveal their most private lives, we often feel compelled to tell all. This isn't always wise. Children, in particular, are seldom ready for all the details, and telling them too much can prove harmful. They need to know only what directly affects them. Telling your seven-year-old boy that you and Daddy are going to live separately is fine, if that's your mutual decision. But giving the same child all the facts will burden him with more than he or she can handle. Your 21-year-old daughter, on the other hand, can be told about the affair; still, the most intimate details need not be revealed.

You can speak to an adult child and say, "Dad and I have decided . . ." and then spell out what the two of you plan to do. You can use such words as "Daddy and I have not been getting along, and I found out he is having an affair with someone else" or "Dad had an affair, and I find that unacceptable" or "Dad had an affair, and we decided to work it out. If sometimes it seems tense in the house, that's what's going on. But whenever you want to talk to either of us about anything, we're both available."

Lurid details are for you alone and are not to be shared with your children. Your hurt, however, cannot be hidden; they will feel and see it anyway. Remember, also, that a child of school age or older may be capable of comforting you, but be careful not to exploit this and use it in an uncaring way.

Rule #4: Never Condemn or Criticize Your Spouse in Front of the Children

When you make disparaging remarks about your spouse to the children, not only might your angry comments come back to haunt you, but they can also cause great damage. When you criticize your spouse to your children, you not only confirm that your marriage has problems, but cause a much more serious difficulty. Adolescents are busy discovering who they are and what they believe. They are moving from a youthful self-centeredness to a more mature sense of moral principles. Able to reason, argue, and be aware of others around them, they are looking for a philosophy of life by which they can truly live. Damning a parent causes anxiety about who they are, and about their sexual and social identifications. Furthermore, it makes children, even in their teens, wonder whether there is anyone they can trust as a role model.

Although your spouse may be a poor role model in your book, he may not be so for the child. Many men and women are poor husbands or wives, but make excellent parents or stimulating and creative mentors. Besides, there may be changes later—in yourself, in your spouse, in the situation—but once you've affixed a label on your spouse, it is not easy to remove. Your child will remember it, and blame you for saying it.

Rule #5: Carefully Select the Words You Use When Speaking to Your Children

Right now you are in an emotional state, so you must make every effort to control the intensity of your feelings until you can speak to your child in a cooler frame of mind. It's fine to talk with an older child about your pain, your anguish, your indecisiveness, your plans; at no age, however, should a child be exposed to screaming, withdrawal, depression, uncontrolled rage, or excessive crying. A young child is terrified by this, and an older child, even a young adult, feels helpless. Seeing a parent in a state of desperation is a terrible scene to witness.

Moreover, children of any age often blame themselves for their parents' troubles. They think, "If only I hadn't done . . . ," "If only I had been . . . ," If only . . . ," "If only . . ." This self-blame creates a wound that takes a long time to heal and can lead to a life of habitual self-blame. It is important, therefore, to be conscious and self-aware. If your mood is one in which you are simply not in control, wait until you have command of yourself, and then speak.

Rule #6: Don't Create a Radically New Persona

Times of crisis can bring out the best in us—and also the worst. Now that you are facing a crisis situation in your marriage, you may find yourself acting quite differently from the way you normally do. You may feel compelled to act as you do, but it's important that you take into account the impact your change may have on your children. Dorothy, who was described earlier, gave this account:

> I was always known to be a quiet, usually genial woman. I liked it that way. No large highs, no great lows. I took it all in stride and played in the middle lane. Then, suddenly this "thing" came along and threw me. I thought, "Where's the payoff for being good? There isn't any!"

So I decided to change. Believe it or not, I started hanging out in bars, nightclubs, discos of a less-than-reputable nature. I picked up guys. My thinking was: "I'll show him!"

Dorothy soon saw what her own shift in behavior was doing to her daughters, aged 9 and 13. To them, Mother had become a different person. They worried about her and, as children are inclined to do, became fiercely protective of her. Parent and child roles were reversed, and the children said such things as, "Mom, you came in so late last night; we thought something had happened to you." The children's concerns finally sank in, and Dorothy saw that she was acting out of character. For the sake of her daughters (and herself), she reclaimed the self she had left behind.

It is important to bear in mind that childhood should be allowed to have its day. That is the purpose behind all of these guidelines. No matter what parents are going through, they must be sensitive to their children's needs. Their response to their children will have a lasting effect.

10

Woman to Woman

Many women, in times of crisis, reach out to a close woman friend. A full 87 percent of married women say that they have their deepest emotional relationship with another woman. Women rely on each other for comfort in an emergency and for daily emotional nourishment. One woman explained:

> My best friend does not condemn or criticize me. She listens. She accepts who I am, where I'm at in my life, and what I feel and want to do about it. Sometimes we don't exchange a word, but I appreciate her presence, and I feel totally, completely understood.

You and your closest friend may have a similar kind of communication that feeds healing.

The Value of Empathy

"I hear her voice and a sea of calm floods me," says Dorothy of her best friend, Ilene. "I don't know what it is, but just a few minutes of talk with her and I'm better. It's as though she has a magic wand, some kind of soothing power. Without her, I couldn't have gotten over the panic I felt when I found out about my husband's affair." Ilene is the reassuring voice that Dorothy needs in times of crisis. She goes on to explain:

> I have a few other friends who also care about me, and I love them. They are fun to be with. We go shopping together, take care of each other's kids, and sometimes go to a matinee or museum. They're a great group of women, but, how can I say it? They're just not Ilene. It's not only that she's intelligent. Most of my friends are smart. It's that she, more than anyone, seems to know what I'm feeling.

Dorothy is talking about the precious quality of empathy—that ability to walk inside someone else's shoes. Dorothy feels that Ilene is on her wavelength, truly understands her. Ilene knows Dorothy as Dorothy knows herself.

The ability to intuit another's emotional state is particularly strong in some people. When you experience a trauma like discovering your husband's affair, you seek out people with this kind of sensitivity. You look for someone who can feel your pain and respond to you with a resonance that makes you feel totally cared about. Such a person seems to hear you from the inside out.

Women As Confidantes

Through the generations, women have chosen other women as confidantes. Men also confide in women (especially their wives). Men say that women seem to understand them more, that they offer more of themselves, and that they are not as afraid of intimacy as men.

Yet, not all women are empathic. For some, the extension of self in order to feel another's pain arouses too much anxiety and conflict. Their response is to run from it all, as in the ancient story of the king who hired a special guard to kick out the poor beggars. The beggars came knocking on his palace door to ask for charity, but he claimed that it broke his heart to see their misery.

A *Case of Missing Empathy*

When Holly was convinced that her spouse was having an affair with one of her colleagues, she sought out her best friend, Marie. The two had been friends since college, when they dated together, took the same classes, and borrowed each other's clothes; Now, married and living a distance apart, they'd seen each other from time to time, meeting along with their husbands as a foursome for dinner. To Holly, Marie had always appeared self-contained, not emotionally volatile like herself. When her husband's affair was revealed to her, she called Marie, sobbing, crying, and talking all at once. She was looking for help, a response that would somehow ease her pain and make her feel better. As Holly tells it:

> I was so surprised. I don't know exactly what I was looking for, but whatever it was, that surely was not it.

There I was, telling Marie that my life was shattered, that I couldn't go on, that my life was a fake. This evil witch had stolen my husband right from under my nose and I, the town idiot, never saw it coming. What would happen to my children, to my family, to *me?* I was ruined forever. If it weren't for the kids, I might end it all. And what did she say in reply? I couldn't believe it—this from my very close friend!

Marie said: "Come on, Holly, don't be so dramatic. It happens to all of us. All men cheat at some time in their lives. It's probably happened to me already, and, if not, it probably will. That's just the way men are." She said that I always overreact; that maybe that's why he had the affair. "No man likes a wife who's always ready to explode," she told me.

Instead of giving Holly the empathy she needed, Marie presented harsh words. She's not a mean person, but Holly's situation made her uncomfortable. Centered in her own feelings, she could not reach out to Holly with genuine understanding. Holly felt dismissed, but she didn't know why Marie would do such a thing.

Rather than seeing Holly, Marie saw a projection of herself. To Holly, this felt like aloofness, criticism, even a sense of disgust. "She pushed me off," Holly said, "as though I were some sort of crazy. After our talk, I felt worse than ever." But a few days later, when Holly had calmed down a little, she realized that she'd simply called the wrong person. Marie was a wonderful friend at college and during dinner dates, but Holly's crisis was more than Marie could handle.

Limits to a Friend's Empathy

Not everyone is adept at being empathic to all who are in need. Some women offer empathy only to the most significant people in their lives, such as close family members. Though they're able to imaginatively sense the experience of others, they seldom choose to extend themselves in this way.

If Holly were to reach out to someone like Susan for empathic understanding, she would most likely be disappointed again. Susan, as we have seen, is cool and aloof; she stays on the periphery of relationships. And if Susan herself were to find out that *her* husband was having an affair, she would probably not call a close woman friend at all. Her tendency is neither to reach out nor to let herself be too deeply affected. Sharing with another is not her style of coping. But if she did reach out, her friend would have to respect her boundaries and not flood her with emotionality. A gentle, reasoned rather than a gushy approach is what feels empathic to Susan.

A Good Friend Is Like a Candle That Always Burns

Betty, who is like an erupting volcano, may seem impervious to empathy, yet she can be reached. When she discovered her husband's affair, she learned what she needed in her friendship with Marilyn. This is how she describes it.

Marilyn and I were three years old when our moms met at our play group. They became friends and so did we. I sometimes think that if she'd had a choice, Marilyn would not have picked me. But we've managed to stay friends all these years despite our many fights. Or should I say *my* fights, because Marilyn's not a fighter. I am, but I never stay mad for long and she knows it. When I do come back and apologize, she accepts me, and I'm always amazed. She's so steady, it's incredible.

I can still remember the night I told her about my husband's affair with a younger woman. I was totally out of my head, in a panic, with this big hole inside me. How could he do such a thing! I called Marilyn, feeling like a kid out of control, spilling my guts while she listened. She told me that what I was feeling made sense, that most women would feel as I did. That calmed me down. She said things like, "Max is wrong in what he did." That also made me feel better. When I told her, sobbing my head off, that I would never get over the affair, she told me that I could call her at any time, day or night, and that she loved me dearly and could feel my pain and anguish.

She offered, then and there, to come over, and she lived an hour away. She said we could go for a walk, or take a ride in the car, or just spend some time talking. God, I felt so much better. Just knowing *she* was *there* made all the difference.

Marilyn gave Betty a place where she could feel secure, safe, and cared about. When Betty was at loose ends, Marilyn's gentleness helped her get a grip on herself. Her caring words were like an anchor. Being with

Marilyn in times of stress is just what Betty needs because the warmth and reassurance bring her back to her center.

Best Friends Are Nonjudgmental

Claire is attentive to the smallest details; she is focused and precise. She concentrates on what she has to do—and does it. In times of crisis, Claire needs a friend who understands her style and who doesn't berate her for being so exacting. Since Claire knows herself well, she's better able to reach out. She knows exactly what she needs, which is why she sought out Tana to help her through the crisis. Tana is an attorney, Claire reasoned, so she's used to being "objective." She knows that intelligence and logic can help arrive at a decision better than screaming and panic can. Claire explained:

> I'm really lucky to have Tana. I knew that, of my three
> best friends, she was the one for me. Immediately she
> asked, "When did it happen and how did you find out?"
> I told her everything I knew, and together we put it into
> one piece. Sometimes I bog down in so much detail, I
> lose the whole picture. Tana helped me put it back in
> perspective. She never judged or criticized me. She was
> clear and to the point. I felt that she really understood
> and took me seriously.

A nonjudgmental friend is a wonderful healer. Being nonjudgmental, in this context, means accepting a friend as she is and supporting her effort to come to terms with the crisis. Here Tana's level-headed but caring approach was a great help in allowing Claire to get on with her life.

Best Friend/Sister

Nancy did not have to go very far to find her best friend. It was her sister Julie. Coming from a family of five daughters, Nancy and Julie had bonded as a team. The two even look alike, although Nancy's hair is long and Julie's is neatly cropped. Even in childhood, when Nancy, the sensitive and vulnerable one, felt hurt, Julie comforted her. She was proud when people mistook them for twins. The two remained very close as adults, so when Nancy found out about her husband's affair, she naturally sought support from Julie. Nancy had been married for seven years and had three children. She was devastated, but Julie really helped:

> Strange how a sister can be a best friend. Julie never puts me down. She cares and would do almost *anything* for me. She really boosts my confidence and gives me support; I couldn't ask for a better friend. I've always trusted her advice.

Different Friends at Different Times

Best friends can be eternal, yet sometimes our choices change. The trauma of a spouse's affair and other periods of exceptional stress call for a friend whose presence you find soothing. The friend you reach out to in shock and pain when the news of the affair first hits you may not be skilled at offering suggestions for healing. Or, the friend may have ideas that don't match your personal style. Let your own response be your guide. A simple question to ask yourself is: "Do I feel better, or do I feel worse?" If you don't feel better, then it's time to make a change. Stay tuned to your own feelings and give them your full respect.

Perhaps you are at a stage where you need some help with decision-making. Should you stay or should you leave? Is this the time to seek professional help? Should you try to get in touch with the "other woman"? A friend who can help you address these questions may be just the one you need. Healing is a stage-by-stage process, and you may need different allies at different phases of the journey.

Guidelines for Choosing a Best Friend Now

Here are some simple guidelines to help you choose the kind of friend you need at each stage of your healing. Remember that although you are under great stress, you still need to make conscious choices. Perhaps these suggestions will help you:

- Be clear about what you *want* and what you *need* at every stage of your healing process.
- As you make decisions about whom to call on, be attuned to your friend's needs, too. Is the person you've chosen capable of dealing with your situation

at this time? If not, move on gracefully to someone
else, with appreciation for anything that the person
you first chose offered.

- As you talk to your best friend, try to be clear as you
translate your feelings into words. Saying "I don't
know; I just feel so lost" may be true, but such statements leave your friend feeling helpless. Instead, tell
her what you want from her. For example: "I need
you to listen to me and help me form a plan of action." Statements like that invite her to be your ally.

The Emotional Contract

Friendship with other women is central to most
women's lives. Women are the people women "come
home to." The emotional contract of nurturing and loving that exists between women friends helps sustain us
through the joys and sorrows of living. At this time of
unusual strain, you may be on the "taking" end of your
friendships; yet you are also "giving" by allowing your
friend to touch your life in meaningful ways. And if at
some time down the road your roles switch, you will
open your heart to receive that special trust from your
friend. This is the unbreakable bond that a woman has
with her best friend—another woman.

11

Heal Yourself

This chapter introduces exercises and techniques to help you make peace with yourself. At this point, taking control of your life and beginning to rid yourself of negative, self-destructive feelings is crucial. You cannot find your way into the future, whether to repair the marriage or seek a new life, unless you are willing to spend some time with (and for) yourself. Furthermore, although it may be difficult to take time from your hectic life, stepping back and calming down is vital. You are going to have to work through whatever decision you make, and therefore need to be in a frame of mind that enables you to do that.

Sorting Out Your Thoughts and Feelings

Negative emotions that are allowed to fester in the psyche can lead to all kinds of illness and dysfunction. Creating a healthy state of mind means clearing out all the energy associated with your painful experience. You can do this by becoming more aware of yourself and becoming a skilled self-observer. This doesn't mean you stop feeling, but rather that you witness your feelings—closely watch your emotions and thoughts as they come and go, stepping aside for the time being so you can see them clearly. Also, learn to distinguish between thoughts and feelings. A thought, as simple as it may sound, is something that you "think." It is in your mind. A feeling, on the other hand, is something you "feel"; it has a more pervasive sense in your body. When we try to "sort out our feelings," we are often just sorting out our thoughts.

Here's an exercise to help you distinguish thoughts from feelings:

> *Stop for a moment and ask yourself: "What am I thinking right now? What's going on in my mind?" Notice where your mind was and then ask: "What am I feeling in my body right now?" Focus only on physical sensations. Survey your body from head to toe; try to be specific about what you notice. Do not generalize about your entire condition as in saying: "I'm tired." Instead, report where you feel tiredness the most. Spend a few minutes in this survey, which is meant to shift your focus away from your thoughts.*
>
> *Now ask yourself: "What emotion am I feeling?" Make sure you are not describing what you are thinking, but rather something you feel. Do not attribute these feelings to anything; simply recognize and feel them. For example, you might say "I'm sad," but avoid thinking why you are sad. The "why" is the thought, the "sad" is the feeling. It is the thought connected to the feeling that stops you from embracing it completely. Learn to sort thinking from feeling. It will leave you with a clearer, more relaxed mind.*

When you actually say to yourself "I'm depressed," "I'm angry," or otherwise acknowledge whatever you feel, you will find that you can think and make decisions in a more rational state of mind. This technique is particularly helpful because it allows you to focus on the here-and-now. It releases you from the hold of the past, with its many recriminations: "But yesterday you said . . . ," "Last month you promised . . . ," and so on. It also keeps you from putting undue focus on the future: "If it isn't finished by next week . . . ," "When you finally decide to do it . . ." Returning a runaway mind to the present puts energy where it's needed and encourages the process of healing.

Visualizations

Your husband's affair is a signal of his own distress in the marriage, and even though you're in pain, you must understand this. Besides his affair, he may turn to other forms of escape, such as alcohol abuse, overeating, or spending long hours on the job. These are clear signs of a dissatisfied mate. Yet despite his anxiety, frustration, or anger, you did not "cause" the affair. He was unwilling or unable to seek your help in changing the marriage; instead, he went outside the relationship for solace. Indeed, the betrayal of your trust undoubtedly galls you the most. To ease this bitter feeling and restore to yourself a sense of personal power, you can use the technique of visual imagery. Psychiatrist Gerald Epstein, in his book *Healing Visualizations*, explains that imagery can help turn negative beliefs into positive ones and, at the same time, strengthen the immune system.

Going Beyond the Betrayal

Here is an exercise to aid you in overcoming your sense of betrayal:

Close your eyes. Exhale fully. Relax. Imagine yourself sitting with your back to your spouse's back. Remember the closeness you felt with him before the affair was exposed. Challenge your reluctance to remember how vulnerable you used to be—how trusting you were. Feel that trust; it's an important part of the healing process. Now breathe out once, fast. Imagine and feel a sharp, stabbing pain in your back. In your mind's eye, imagine turning and looking directly into your husband's face. Let yourself fully feel the pain, humiliation, and sense of betrayal that felt like a knife in your back. Stay with the pain long enough to feel it to your core.

Exhale fully. Extend your arm around your back and visualize removing the symbolic blade of betrayal. Turn around toward your spouse. Look at his face. See his tears of remorse and, with your extended hand, touch his cheek, moistening your fingers with his tears. Reach your hand behind your back and apply his tears to the gaping knife wound. Imagine a golden glow that spreads across the wound as it closes and heals. Feel, sense, and know that you are enveloped in a soft golden healing light. Inhale deeply; open your eyes.

Do this exercise twice a day, for a full week. Repeat it whenever you feel yourself entrapped in the negative feelings. If it is too difficult to do on your own, ask a friend to quietly sit with you. The exercise will change and soften the way you are thinking and feeling.

Getting Back on Your Feet

You may also feel that you've lost your balance and can't get back on your feet, that your world has been turned upside-down. It's a lot like having the rug pulled out from under you. Here is an exercise to restore your sense of having both feet on the ground:

Close your eyes. Exhale fully. See yourself standing on a rug. Pay attention to its size, color, and design. Feel, sense, and know a power trying to pull the rug out from under you. Feel yourself stumble, scrambling to maintain your balance. Sense your fear of falling. Now blow out a fast, short burst of air. Imagine that your breath can blow long, powerful spikes into each corner of the rug, securing the rug in place. Notice that the spikes are giving off a golden glow that suffuses the rug. Know now that you are on solid ground. Feel, sense, and know that no one can pull the rug out from under you.

Opening Up to Life

You may think that, because of your husband's affair, you will never trust anyone again. The very thought of being so vulnerable is frightening. Yet healing requires that you open yourself to life once more. Here is an exercise to help you do that:

Close your eyes. See yourself as a lone flower bud on a bush. You are closed very tightly and exposed to the harsh elements. Feel the cold stiffen you. Feel the rain soak you. Feel the wind buffet you against the branches. Know that you are lonely, tired, and scared. Exhale fully. Feel the

*wind become a soft breeze. Feel the rays of the sun dry
your dampness. Slowly, slowly begin to open your petals
to the warmth of the sun. Birds are singing. Other flowers
are blooming beside you. Open fully as the sun warms
you. Notice what color you are. Know that you are safe in
the sunlight. Open your eyes.*

Regaining Self-Confidence

Another reaction that you might have to your husband's
infidelity is the sense that you have lost your femininity.
A rival has entered the picture, and you wonder, "Is she
more beautiful than I am?" You need to reclaim your
own special beauty and let go of painful comparisons.
This exercise will help to restore self-confidence:

*Close your eyes. Exhale deeply. See a kindly spirit waving
her magic wand over you. Light emanates from the wand
and spreads around the room, dissipating the shadows.
Follow your guide as she leads you to a closet, inside of
which you find some beautiful garments to wear. Arrange
your hair in the way that pleases you most, and feel yourself glowing with beauty. Look at yourself in the full-
length mirror, find the beauty in you, and see a golden
light all around you. Breathe in deeply. Your inner radi-
ance shines through, and it's lovely to behold. Now, gently
open your eyes.*

Letting Go of Anger

When you have been hurt, deeply hurt, it is difficult to
forgive, but forgiveness is a balm to both giver and

receiver. To forgive is to accept the other, and yourself, without blame. In order to do that, you must let the resentment leave you. You may fear that once you let go of the anger, there will be nothing left, but this exercise on forgiveness addresses that:

> *Close your eyes. Exhale fully. See your heart. Feel and know its pain. Feel it bursting with bitterness and anger. See the bitterness and anger straining to leave your heart. Exhale and release. Open your heart. Feel, see, and know that the bitterness is leaving. Know that your heart has been emptied of its bitterness. Feel your heart, sad and empty. See yourself and your partner sharing a promise to forgive one another. See yourself and your partner move toward your open heart. See your heart invite you and your partner deep inside. Feel the beauty of the open heart. Open your eyes.*

This exercise is helpful regardless of what you plan to do, whether you choose to remain in the marriage or to seek a new life. Either way, you will need to begin with an open heart, free of the burden of bitterness and anger.

Repairing Family Ties

If your partner is truly remorseful and wants to heal the wound, you may decide to repair the marriage together. Knowing that his family ties have been seriously damaged, he may wish to make restitution. This visualization exercise will help him:

Close your eyes. Exhale fully. See yourself alone. Feel your isolation and pain. Ahead of you, in the distance, see your family and community at a dinner table. Each person is breaking off a piece of bread. See an empty space beside your spouse. Feel and know your estrangement, distance, and guilt. Exhale and release. See sunlight pouring through a window. The sunlight is guiding you. Walk to the table and take your seat. As the bread is passed to you, break off a piece. Put it in your mouth and taste it. Feel, sense, and know that you are welcomed back into the community. Feel, sense, and know that you are in your rightful place.

Guided Meditation

A guided meditation is like an extended visualization, and it can help you find a place of refuge in yourself. All of us need a safe environment where we feel loved and protected, and the following journey takes you to the realm of safety within yourself:

Sit in a comfortable position with your legs uncrossed and your feet on the floor. Close your eyes. Inhale deeply. As you exhale, slowly release the tension that you are holding in your chest. Take another, slower, deeper breath and, as you exhale, feel your body relaxing even more. Continue breathing at a slow, comfortable pace.

Picture yourself seated comfortably on the porch of a small cabin in the woods. Notice the beautiful mixture of fall colors and evergreen trees. Smell the fresh fall air and feel the warmth of the afternoon sun on your face and hands. It is very peaceful. Picture yourself rising from your seat to take a walk in the beautiful woods. See yourself walking across the porch, going down the steps, and heading toward the path that leads into the trees. Hear the leaves and pine needles softly crunching under your feet as you walk, and smell the distinctive essences of the various trees as you enter the forest.

Notice, as you walk, that you are drawn to a path that goes up a gentle hill toward a favorite place of yours. Walk up the path, feeling your easy stride. Listen to the forest sounds—the rustling leaves, the singing birds, the gently blowing breeze. Notice how the sun filters through the trees. Smell the air. As you finish the climb, see yourself entering a clearing with a pool of spring-fed water. Walk toward it and kneel by the water's edge. Notice your reflection in the crystal-clear water. Reach down and scoop up some water in the palm of your hand. Feel its coolness; taste how delicious it is.

Sit down by the water and feel yourself enjoying this sacred spot. As you rest, notice that you are aware of a divine figure slowly approaching. Look toward the woods and see this beautiful being emerge. See the loving light in the being's eyes. Rise up to meet your guide and feel the safety of his or her presence. Pay attention to your inner voice as the being says, kindly, that it will look at some of your fears with you today if you are ready. Listen closely for your answer while the divine presence offers you a protective shield. Reach out and take the shield, if you want to use it.

Go to the edge of the water with your divine guide and feel the gentle touch of his or her hand on your *shoulder. Look down into the pool and see that the water has become a sort of movie screen and that you can see yourself in your daily life as if you were watching a video. Your divine guide will choose for you, if you have given permission, the fears that you will look at today. You may ask your guide to show you any fears that you may have about the changing cycle in your marriage. Look into the water and see if anything else is there for you to view. You may also ask whether you need to look at any fears about the changing state of your health today. Look into the water for the answer.*

You may ask your guide whether you need to look at any other fears of change today. Look into the water and see what it holds.

Now thank your guide for showing you these things and for being with you today. Gently say good-bye. Return to the cabin along the same path you took earlier. Feel yourself walk peacefully down the hill. Notice the changing light, as it is now late afternoon. Walk back toward the clearing around the cabin. Feel the cooler air as evening comes on. Approach the cabin, climb the steps, and again sit comfortably on the porch. Now think back over the journey you have just taken. Acknowledge any fears you saw, and know that you have the strength and courage to deal with them. Gently bring the scene to a close. Then, when you are ready, open your eyes and fully remember your experience.

Set Your Face to the Future

These exercises will help you find your way back to your core self—that inner self that houses the treasure chest of happiness, balance, love, and joy. Such emotions may be hard for you to recognize right now, for betrayal has seared you with pain. Yet your experiences have shown you that both good and bad are part of life's offerings. When your pain is acute, you feel as though it's the total of your experience, but pain can dissolve if you are willing to let it go. New life always comes with the dissolution of the old. Without letting go, nothing new can appear. When you feel calm and soothed, you can make a conscious choice, one that comes from your wisdom and your caring for yourself.

Throughout this book, you have learned about yourself and the man you married. You know the possibilities for healing the marriage, and if you feel love and a sense of hope for it, your choice is clear. You both must do everything you can to reestablish trust. You must also learn to interpret the affair as a wake-up call, a signal that your relationship was built on shaky ground. Finally you must also see that this experience, as painful as it may be, can lead the two of you to a true "we" based on trust, friendship, and a deeply committed love.

The Final Ingredient

One strategy for loving often gets overlooked—positive reinforcement. Though we all know we can build strength by focusing on positive aspects, we often forget.

To experience intimacy—real intimacy as a couple—you need to share the love of each other's total self—the joys and the pains, the laughter and the grief.

Typically, when problems arise between you, conversations seem to focus on "working it out." But as the phrase suggests, such efforts feel like "work," which is tedious. When a couple faces a relationship crisis, it's important that you not equate every contact with tedium. It is essential that you weave pleasure into the communication. Remind yourselves why you're in the relationship in the first place. Celebrate!

How long has it been since you last celebrated something with each other? Sure, you have lots of problems that taint your closeness; anger and pain have gotten in the way. You're perfectly willing to spend hour after hour talking about the bad stuff, the problems—how you feel disappointed or betrayed by your love partner. But what about the good stuff you have together; the very fact that you *are* together, the fact that this tragedy did *not* automatically separate you, as it might have other people. Celebrate the fact that you are both still here, searching for solutions! Tell your husband that you want to go out with him, do something special, simply to celebrate that you have each other:

- Celebrate your connection
- Celebrate your friendship
- Celebrate the fact that your souls touch each other
- Celebrate your love

The husband of a 78-year-old woman died after they had been married for 55 years. She and he had a beautiful relationship because they always celebrated their love. They weathered many storms together, including his affair; but they got through it, and all along continued to celebrate their love. Even during times of intense anger and betrayal, they kept the promise to go out to dinner once a week at a new place and not talk about problems. Every week they found a new restaurant and had a small split of champagne with which they toasted each other.

After he died, she was understandably heartbroken, but her spirit stayed intact. Each week she bought a split of champagne and went to the grave and toasted "my Bernie," as she called him. She would bring two glasses, drink hers, and spill his on his grave. She also brought a flower. She did this for the remaining nine years of her life and stayed vibrant and happy. Imagine seeing someone at a gravesite with flowers and champagne, toasting the love that remains in her or his heart for the person who died.

Imagine that feeling between you and your husband. Imagine it, and you can make it happen. Celebrate the impossibility of your relationship—how you found each other in this haystack of humanity. Celebrate the changes. Think of where you were at the beginning, think of how unreal it was, think of how much more real it is now.

Celebrate how each of you have faced your own inner demons to be with each other. Celebrate how strong each of you were to survive the damages of the past. Celebrate the fact that you survived to the point where you are now, no matter how bad it looks, no matter how rotten you're feeling at this particular time.

Imagine a woman having a problem with her husband. It looks like their relationship is dead, they haven't had sex for ages, and she can barely talk to him without getting angry or crying. Now imagine that she comes home to a person who has a table set with flowers and dance music playing as she walks in the door. He says, "I thought we'd have a little celebration tonight, a celebration of the fact that although we're going through the roughest of times, we have had each other all these years and we still have each other now!"

Imagine having this offered to you. Would you even know how to receive it? Would you automatically distrust it—thinking he had an ulterior motive? What a pity! You know why that would happen? Because you didn't celebrate enough with each other in the past and you forgot how important it was—and is. Following are guidelines to help you and your spouse celebrate your marriage:

- Pick one aspect you want to celebrate.
- Get a blank card and personalize it (Congratulations to us for . . .).
- Make a plan to celebrate.
- Have a party for two.
- Go on a date.
- Do it outside or inside your home, but make it special.
- Light candles and dress up.
- Turn on the music and dance together.
- Decorate with flowers.
- Do as you would do when celebrating someone's birthday.
- Be in good spirits.

- Postpone bad news.
- Refrain from practical discussion.
- Make a toast to the thing you're celebrating.
- Celebrate your existence in each other's life.
- Make the evening magical. (Realize that having each other at all is magic!)
- Celebrate something in the *now* rather than the future.
- Talk about what *is* instead of what isn't!
- Spend time in silence.
- Touch.
- Smile.
- Set aside time for your celebration at least once each week.

Celebrating your marriage together will make all the difference.

Index